I'm Limping Very Well, Thank You

Mind. Mood. Motivation.

W. Nicholas Abraham, M.Div., Ph.D.

drnick@nickabraham.net
www.nickabraham.net

Acknowledgments

Books just don't happen. Much like the new structure I watched from my window for the past year being built across the street, this book came together in stages. There were foundational writings that focus on self: self-direction, self-limitation, self-control and self-awareness. The roof was an important part of the book, the umbrella if you will, of self-protection that helps us weather the storms of life. Then came the walls that help us realize when an issue is about my behavior and when it belongs in another room. Soon after the lighting and the plumbing were installed, issues which brighten our pathway, insights that provide cool water for the journey and challenges that give hot water to soothe life's injustices.

Lastly, and perhaps most importantly, came the interior. What can we create from what we've been given through reflection upon our life development? How and when do our walls need to be transformational? And when do they need to be concrete? To what degree will placement of our emotions decorate life or take away from its external beauty? What colors will we use to bring calm and harmony to our violent world? When will we have to realize that some of the technological foundation on which we build our lives is shifting at a profound speed? To what degree will the attitude affect those who enter through our doorway? And at what point will we open the doors of our hearts with humility, accepting all who come in as they are and not as we would have them?

This book just didn't happen, and much like any supposed

expert in his or her respective field, this book is the product of many years of being a wounded mental health professional, a poor beggar looking for spiritual food and a human person, seeking to continually learn how to navigate through this wonderful thing we call life.

I dedicate this work to my Father, who after 87 years of life, died on February 18, 2014. It was after his death that I decided to complete this project and give it to the world in his honor.

For truly, he was and still is the most honorable man I have ever known.

Gretchen Herrmann, Cover art and design
Mindy Brodhead Averitt, Editor

Table of Contents

I'm Limping Very Well, Thank You 7
Staying on My Mat 12
Keeping Our No's Clean 16
I'm Worth More 22
A Call to Arms: The Healing Ones 26
A Modern-Day Prayer 32
Amusing Ourselves to Life 35
Positivity and Certainty: Within Reach 40
A Priceless Letter 44
Creating a Drama-Free Zone 48
A Season for Burning Bridges 52
Cuddling with Our Demons 57
Reasonable Happiness 62
On Stings and Things 66
7:17 a.m. 71
Sometimes I Sits and I Thinks 75
Bullying: Uncovering the Cause 78
Bullying: Love is the Answer 83
From Too Much to Not Enough 88
Fouls, Flags and Playing within the Guidelines of Life 93
The Voice of Abiding Love 98
Water Your Own Grass 108
Why Forgiveness Matters 110
Hallmarks of the Real Self 113
Slow Down 117
Vulnerability, Authenticity and Humility 121
Choose to Refuse to Excuse 126
From Betrayal to Forgiveness 131
Christmas: A Season for Higher Standards 136
A Counter-Culture Christmas 141
Angel of Death or Angel of Grace? 144
The Waiting Game 149
The Gift of Grief 155
The Murder of Matthew Shepard 159
Technology Has Gone Public 164
Film Not Made for Theater 168
Rights and Responsibilities 172
A Bucket List that Will Change Your Life 176

I'm Limping Very Well, Thank You

"... I've learned that I set the standard, no one else; that neither approval of others nor job stability nor even good health are worthy prayers. I'd rather continue to be receptive to what comes my way..."

Depression. I've been there. Many of us have. But to conclude with "I've bought the t-shirt" would only further disenfranchise what is already voiceless. Silence of the soul becomes the ever-present stream of consciousness while roars of worthlessness crowd the prison of despair.

There is no light in depression; only darkness. Ironically, there is no darkness in depression; only blinding light. There is no path out of depression; only bushes and mud through which to wade. There is no magic prescription or 28-day program that overcomes the toxins of hopelessness.

The passing of seconds seems like days. Being told "this too shall pass" is a trumpet without sound. And the smell of morning's dew is nauseating. Anguish overcomes all purpose and desire.

Depression is cunning and quiet. Our bodies are not elevated off of the bed; there is no neck turning. We don't become grotesque and destructive to others. No. The possession is internal. It is as if we are in a jail cell: a lifetime sentence with a constant and fiendish bully that feeds on our desperation. And we can't kill the bully without killing the victim.

For anyone who may think that death's allure is monstrous and cowardly, let me assure them that a death sentence would at times be a welcome release from the fear of constant torture.

Depression is so complex that we can't say with any degree of certainty whether it is a brain disease, a drug-related disease or an environmental disease. Whether it is a passing down from previous generations or a throwing up of childhood trauma, a mental disease or a spiritual battle.

We only know that unlike cancer which cannot kill the soul, depression can. Unlike a sinus infection that can be cured with antibiotics, depression can't.

Depression is a predator that feeds off of itself until there is no ability to act and which paradoxically, can only be defeated through action. And herein lies the hope of caring for if not curing depression.

It may not ever be cured, but it can be managed. And just as one limps through life with one leg longer than the other, one can learn to walk with the limp from depression.

The only true course out of the woods is through the body and mind holding hands and dragging each other along, limping all the way.

When I was experiencing a deep and dark depression more than 20 years ago, I was taking an anti-depressant and working toward my doctorate. My memory is still intact.

I had friends and family who loved me and never gave up on my ability to find some way out or, should I say, some way into the world of peace and joy. I had people who pushed me to get out of bed at a certain time each day, to force myself to eat healthily and to walk two miles a day. I had a brother and sister who came to visit me when I was in treatment and who sat next to me when I spoke of wanting to die, who accepted me as I was, a broken and endangered species. They showed me that they, too, had fears, dark nights, loneliness and despair. That the human condition was not about an absence of suffering, but about the presence of God within me.

I vividly recall when I was released from treatment, they took me to see *Jurassic Park*, and even though I was in torment for most of the movie, I remember being out of my prison for a few minutes and the feeling of oxygen coming into my body.

I recall a friend who met me on a bench at Marquette with a bottle of water and a sandwich and told me to eat. I stared into space and with tears, attempted to open the sandwich wrapper. I didn't have the energy to accomplish that. Instead of making a fuss, my friend opened the sandwich and told me that it was okay. I just needed to eat, regardless of what I felt.

The days were long, and there were nights when I watched the clock, hour after hour, until it was time to face another day. I remember how lonely I felt when I walked into my apartment and that neither alcohol nor a visit to a bar would remedy that feeling. So I would sit at the piano or the guitar, and sometimes I would write or call someone. But mostly, I would think about how my future was not lost and that I could make a profound change, even if it meant becoming homeless. Yes, even that was better than continuing to live the way I had been since high school: running from myself.

As I began to breathe through my own body and not those around me, I began to feel like a transplanted tree whose roots were real and growing. Acts of kindness towards others fed similar acts toward myself. Exercise, nutrition, goals and helping others without fanfare were cleansing my soul.

I recall a few months later, a trip to Nashville to see my brother led to a comedian in my presence cracking jokes and, out of nowhere, a smile appeared, the first in many months.

I remember going to a picnic in Chicago and taking a very large strawberry pie to be shared by a dozen people. And how it rained on us – poured, in fact – as we were about to eat. I voiced loudly, "Pull out your umbrellas and eat up, everyone. I am not going to see this pie go to waste." And how during that moment of assertiveness, I was experiencing certainty and passion.

They say that the older and deeper a depression is, the longer it takes to come through it. I say that there is no such thing as really coming through it.

To this day, I live with both the memories and the threat of a recurrence. As we say of cancer, it's in remission. But I am still taking my medication. I have since changed careers, discerned friendship choices and taken on a new perspective towards my wonderful family and parents, whom I wanted to blame for my pain during those turbulent years.

I've become astute when it comes to ascertaining atmospheres that are toxic to my soul and, for the most part, I steer clear of them and, when confronted with something threatening to my well-being, I duck and run with no shame, guilt or remorse. I've learned that flight is sometimes a wonderful choice to make, and that I'm much happier when I am not trying to convince, argue with, convert or defend.

I am singing again, writing with my own words and thoughts, and learning how to cope without the wonder drugs and other forms of entertainment that leave me more lonely than before. I am learning to look to a power greater than the storms of life and to feel compassion and concern for those people who once intimidated me.

Mostly, I have learned that authenticity is the most fruitful pathway in life, despite what may be said about me. In fact, I've accepted that what people say is none of my business. I've learned that I set the standard, no one else; that neither approval of others nor job stability nor even good health are worthy prayers. I'd rather continue to be receptive to what comes my way, with confidence that I can smile with gratitude, even at the angel of death.

I've learned through my illness that I am the best navigator of my boat, that I like my little boat and that I don't have to navigate the boats around me or compare my boat to the yachts that pass me by. At times, I may have to be alert so that I am not blindsided by one, but for the most part, navigation of my boat through both the calm and the storm is what makes life challenging. And that I am up to the challenge.

I've learned that navigation is more about acting than thinking. I look toward what's ahead and move the feet and attitude in a certain direction, fearing only that my little boat will at some point give out. But even then, it will have been a journey well worth it. Because it was my journey, my experience, my judgment. And whatever came as a result of my travels, life became more valuable as a result of the limp, not in spite of it.

Staying on My Mat

"... now is the time we all stay on our own mat and not become too fixated on fixing anyone, comparing ourselves to anyone, judging anyone, searching to score political points with anyone."

Recently, a dear friend invited me to a yoga seminar. According to her invitation, I would be hearing one of the gurus of the world of yoga and would be very inspired, if not by the movement itself, certainly by his words.

I went somewhat begrudgingly, concerned more that I would be one of a few novices and spend the evening becoming self-conscious among the great many experts. My friend met me at the door, gave me a mat and told me to simply let the experience happen, wiping out any and all expectations for the next two hours.

Naturally, after seeing more than 60 people, dressed immaculately in yoga garb (whatever that is) and reminding me of the day I chose a graduate course as an undergraduate and the resulting feeling I had among the intelligentsia, I chose a spot against the back wall. Such a spot would allow me some safety from the forces of the secret society I had entered.

The lecture went on for approximately 45 minutes, and I was mesmerized by the speaker's candor, humility and, most of all, earthiness. His language would have been offensive to some, and his style would have made anyone wonder what on earth the $60 per person was all about. A con job, no doubt. But not so. He drew me in like a cool swimming pool on a deep South August day. My only regret was that I wasn't able to take notes. And there were so many pearls that I could never remember them all. But the theme was pure and without stain: "People bring their crap to yoga, and what happens is that yoga is turned into crap."

From there, he had me. Yoga was not about transforming or fixing or healing: He wasn't about to let we from the West look for the end result first. In fact, it was clear to this wisdom figure that the search for the end was our basic problem. Within the hour, I had become calmer and, while a bit uncomfortable on the floor, kept my eyes on the prize, which turned out to be quite opposite of what I had expected.

We began the yoga 50 minutes into the evening, and I regressed immediately. Looking around, wondering if I was looking the part, doing it the right way, anxiously hoping someone would stop and take breaks (so that I could) and fully convinced that he was watching this pathetic creature butcher what was so dear to his heart. And then the miracle happened.

He asked us to cease the exercise and take the yoga sitting position. Terrified, I almost walked out when he began his questioning. He asked how many of us were looking around, wondering if we were doing it right. How many were seeking out the people to watch for the proper form and wondering if he was singling each of us out with hidden laughter or worse, disgust? At that moment, I began to experience a profound inner peace. It didn't matter if anyone else had gotten caught with the hammer in hand, beating my poor 57-year-old body with "should." I realized that this truly was a guru.

He asked us to cease and desist of such meanderings and simply listen to our bodies and focus on our abilities, limitations and execution of our own unique form. He asked us to take breaks as needed, to feel our toes, knees, legs, arms, facial tension and to allow the stretching of the body to be enough. In essence, he asked us to simply "stay on our mat" and stop bothering with everyone else's. It was an amazing gift, an astonishing yet totally freeing allowance that had me back in the safety of my own home, literally being in my body and no one else's.

When we got back into the class, I did precisely what I was asked, not because the teacher said to, but because I knew that he was absolutely on target. He was asking each of us to be our own expert, our own mystic, our own master of the little bit of life that the Universe had given us to steward.

At the end of the class, another miracle occurred. I came out of the trancelike state of self and body focus and sat on the mat that was "mine" for the evening, and I became aware that in the room were more than 60 other human beings sitting on their mats. We were a community of individuals who were living out our own self-made film in the company of other sojourners. I felt a bond with these people like none other, and to this day, even though I met only a few of them afterwards, feel that we are a part of each other and that our combined energy had made the world a little better place in which to live.

Perhaps now is the time we all stay on our own mat and not become too fixated on fixing anyone, comparing ourselves to anyone, judging anyone, searching to score political points with anyone. Perhaps we simply focus on what we each have been given in life and how wonderful life really is when we stay on our own mat and focus on our own resources.

When I came out of the yoga exercise that night, I was more grateful than I had ever been. And it was because I was aware of my body and my life, and I was extremely grateful for the lives of those in the room with me.

To this day, I tell this story to my clients. I tell them that this is obviously not an advertisement for yoga. It is an advertisement for life, and I remind them, as well as myself, that with each day that comes, so does the healthy and loving attitude of staying on one's own mat.

Keeping Our No's Clean

"No one really likes to say No. We like to say Yes because we are made for service. We are hard-wired to help. It's in our nature to be pleasing."

The Terrible 2s evoke memories of the dreaded sound of No!, an utterance as pervasive as Southern summer humidity. Toddlers and stubbornness travel in pairs. The egocentric world roars as desire develops.

Watch little people on their journey to use their powers, grabbing everything in sight as if they were the creators of the world, and you'll know that having the freedom to move without restraint is an essential human drive. But so, too, is frustration. Little people learn quickly to say No! when they don't like being separated from or blocked. They experience the world as restrictive. And they don't like it.

The larger power, a more ominous Goliath that seeks to frustrate unbridled movement, clashes with the tiny David. And in this epic war for survival, Goliath always wins.

Reflect on this, and you'll realize one's self-image has been affected by such a marvelous, self-made movie, and it has contributed to our default buttons as we balance separateness with intimacy and self-assurance with the need for love and approval.

With this quest in mind, I began to ask people what it felt like to say No!, to reject a request that goes against their value system, to turn away from gossip, to avoid another family member's drama, to honor a prior commitment by passing up a better invitation, to deny a personal favor, to forsake a friend's need for a higher need, to end an unhealthy friendship, to say No! to a worn-out lifestyle, a behavior that is self-abusive or a job that is no longer fulfilling.

The answers followed a universal pattern. No one really likes to say No. We like to say Yes because we are made for service. We are hard-wired to help. It's in our nature to be pleasing. But that's not the only motive.

We also fear the response – the consequence – from the outer power that still appears to be larger than us. We fear for our reputation, our image, our stature, our ability to survive. It's as if without thinking, we draw from the well of life as a 2 year old and we ready ourselves for a struggle over where the line is drawn. Without much thought about whom I need to help more, myself or the other, whom I need to serve more, myself or the other, we automatically default to what we "Should do."

We take one of the following courses:
   1) avoiding an answer;
   2) saying yes and then aborting the process by not following through;
   3) saying yes and harboring bitterness; or
   4) saying yes out of guilt, fear, an overly inflated power to save or a highly developed sense of obligation.

While I suspected that giving a No! would not be easy for people, more eye-opening was what people did after they said No! The word always carried an explanation, judgment or self-incrimination. It appeared to me that when we do say No, we have to give a commentary on why. We explain that we can't because of (fill in the blank) and make sure we defend the response so as to not offend the other. To simply say No or No thank you is never sufficient. A wall of explanation goes up immediately.

Yes, it's true that people often ask, "Why?" when a No is uttered, which only serves to push us into explanations and, unfortunately, too often a lie. We can't seem to say the real reason for the No, so we come up with an excuse, a lie, anything to block the ensuing drama.

And then there's the other side of No. It's when we say No out of a history of co-dependency or, if you will, a pattern of saying Yes when we didn't want to but were addicted to the all-encompassing "need to be loved" and "fear of being abandoned." We carry and harbor resentment over a history of saying Yes, and it eventually takes us down to the hell of "door matting." Trust me, hell really hath no fury like a person who has said to Yes to everyone else all of her life, leaving the needs of the self-starved for attention.

But when trampled on enough, the toddler roars, Foul! The newly found victim finds a renewed sense of power, and rage is created.

What could be a simple No becomes,
    "No, I will not clean up your mess."
    "No, I will not continue to enable that behavior."
    "No, I will not be your crutch or your drug or your savior or your slave."
    "No, I will not forgive your drinking anymore. I'm done."
    "No, it's not me. It's you who is the problem."

Notice a pattern? It's not just a No. It's a judgmental No. It's a No that has to somehow put the other person down, punish the other, make it known that it's not just No. It's a No that is steeped in resentment and past wounds, either felt for the event/person of the moment or, more often and more sinister, the painful "door matting" of our past.

Let's face the hard fact. It's just hard to say No and leave it at that. We are programmed early on to either justify the raising of our drawbridge because we fear the consequences of No, or worse, dropping it on those to whom in the past we have given of ourselves and whom now we call invaders and robbers.

Underneath the fear of saying No was the core message underneath the explanation. People who are uncomfortable saying No admitted that they felt inadequate, and saying No meant they could not meet another's needs and that they Should be able to. Saying No, instead of being a simple acceptance of one's personal limits and responsibilities, became a shaming signal that set off feelings from long ago that one should always be there, on alert, available, giving, helping, fixing, supporting, providing, enabling, correcting or worse, used to medicate someone else's pain. By saying No, we admit that we are limited and at times powerless. And so the explanation, even the judgment, helps to cover the feeling of inadequacy.

Ironically, No's with judgment in the wings are indeed a way of getting back at and making others feel inadequate; of throwing bitterness around, of making sure that new boundaries are reset by clearly stating "not anymore." Anger and rage at times accompanied the No, and by screaming at the world, one was actually screaming at all of the many times in the past when they couldn't say No, when they didn't have the courage or the power to draw the line in the sand out of self-respect.

Yet those who rediscovered the power of No in their journeys to recovery, a simple word that carried more force than any Iron Man or Thor could ever muster, found that it need not come from the frustration of a 2 year old but from the interior reign of an adult. A force that was rooted in one's core being.

Think about the times when you neither fought, defended, lashed out, judged nor explained. You simply said No, and in doing so, said Yes to your own needs. You felt taller, walked more confidently and slept better. You may have lost friends and the world you had grown accustomed to, but in the moment of saying it, you knew the end was actually the beginning. With a simple No, one is saying, "I don't want to," and the sky doesn't fall.

Keeping the No clean and simple cleanses and simplifies one's life.

It's not that saying No makes life any more pleasurable. But it does make it more authentic, more self-aware and self-assured. In keeping No's clean, we discover that others will get what they need from a power greater than us. And that is the essence of true faith. When we respectfully and joyfully say, "No, I am not God," we applaud our humanity and enjoy peace.

These are the times when we speak most deeply from integrity, when we respond to the world through a simple word that means we neither live in, for nor through others, for we are all passing through this world. It means we do live in, for and through ourselves and in our own unique world. It is then when, only with confidence in and not hatred of a larger power within us, we can find a resting place.

Augustine once said, "Our hearts are restless until they rest in Thee." In my humble opinion, he was half-right. Our hearts also rest in, for, with and through our very selves.

Such is one of the most precious assets of being human, and no principalities or powers should ever be allowed to take that away.

There is, indeed, much power in saying No. And even more power when it needs no explanation, justification or judgment. For then the "Yes to Self" can keep on giving from within, where Jesus once said the Kingdom of God resides.

I'm Worth More

" ... our worth is what drives us. When our worth is being tested, like gold, we have the opportunity to increase our value with every choice."

Several years ago, when I was working with the military in Japan, I was overtaken and humbled by the Japanese people's customary greeting. The person I was introduced to would make eye contact and bow for a few seconds before me, as if I were royalty.

Here in the West, when we go in front of the holy of holies (or at least Catholics do), we genuflect. In the East, they bow, recognizing those they meet as a "holy of holies." We also have a tendency to misunderstand the notion that we are not worthy during many of our religious rituals, mistaking the notion of unworthiness as damaged by our environment as well as our actions. Such falsehoods have pervaded our society, and it's high time we reset the inner computer, replacing the old software with a bow instead of a kneel, a love of self instead of self-loathing and a response to the world that says, "I am worth more, and so are you."

When I meet someone, I want to bow before them and recognize their dignity, their honor, their value in my presence. I want to notice each and every person as holy and the ground upon which they walk as having been made holier through their touch. When I work with people in my office, I wish to help them see their higher selves, their greater potential, their best choices and judgments. I wish to enable them to trust themselves, respect themselves and enjoy the limited chances we have to love and be loved.

Those experiences have led me to reflect upon the reality

that we are indeed worthy of love, respect, compassion, dignity and our contribution to the fabric of our earthly existence. First and foremost, we are worth more than we could ever imagine.

Such a gift comes with challenges and responsibilities that even the strongest among us find a struggle. Nonetheless, our worth is what drives us. When our worth is being tested, like gold, we have the opportunity to increase our value with every choice.

Therefore:
- When you are drawn into the world of gossip, bow to the world and say, "I am worth more, and so are you."
- When you are on the edge of being negative, bow to your better self and say, "I am worth more, and so are you."
- When you are comparing the here and now to yesterday, bow to today and say, "I am worth more, and so are you."
- When you are tempted to use a substance, bow to the greater pleasure of serenity and say, "I am worth more, and so are you."
- When you are stressed and need a quick fix, bow to the gift of tomorrow and say, "I am worth more, and so are you."
- When you are focused only on yourself and having a pity party, bow to the world of service and say, "I am worth more, and so are you."
- When you are judged by those who are insecure and looking for a scapegoat, bow to them and say, "I am worth more, and so are you."
- When you can't find a way out of a problem, bow to acceptance and say, "I am worth more, and so are you."

- When you hear a voice that says you aren't good enough, bow to your creator, stop and say, "I'm worth more, and so are you."
- When you are tempted to climb the ladder of success at the risk of losing your soul, bow to integrity and say, "I am worth more, and so are you."
- When the road ahead is foggy and filled with frightening noises, bow to faith over sight and say, "I am worth more, and so are you."
- When your parents say you are hurting their image because you are gay, bow to their fear and say, "I am worth more, and so are you."
- When your child of 17 is doing drugs and you are inclined to bear the shame of guilt, bow to her dignity and say, "I am worth more, and so are you."
- When every door has closed and you are sitting in the darkness of confusion, bow to your solitude and say, "I am worth more, and so are you."
- When you feel the need for approval from others, bow to your dignity and say, "I am worth more, and so are you."
- When you are accused falsely, bow to truth and say, "I am worth more, and so are you."
- When others attack you and call you names, bow to the spirit of compassion and say, "I am worth more, and so are you."
- When you lose a job or find out that someone else has been hired, bow to divine providence and say, "I am worth more, and so are you."
- When you've lost a loved one and feel that life is meaningless, don't beat yourself up. Stop and say, "I am worth more, and so are you."
- When your dreams have turned into ashes and all you have lived for is gone, stop and say, "I am worth more, and so are you."

- When your eyes are dirtied by pornography, your mind becomes dusty from alcohol and your heart is sullied from using others, stop and say, "I am worth more, and so are you."
- When you have given up on God, others and even yourself, stop and say, "I am worth more, and so are you."

You are worth more than the number of followers on Twitter. More than the shoes in your closet. More than the medications you take.

You are worth more than the work you produce. More than the Shopping Network can provide. More than the car you drive or the house in which you dwell.

You are worth more than the reputation you have, the fears you dwell in and the parties to which you are invited.

You are worth more than your salary, your degrees, your anxieties.

You are in fact, priceless. There is no way to calculate your worth in worldly terms because you don't measure your life by worldly standards: They will come and go, soon to pass away, but you are eternal.

You are your own best friend and worst enemy. You are your most favored companion, for you live with yourself 24 hours a day. You are a gift to the world in all of your multiple pathways and personas, and only you can decide your value. Stop and say, "I'm worth more than even my self-appraisal."

A Call to Arms: The Healing Ones

"... We live for pills more than for fruit, for diagnosis more than for mystery, for getting fixed more than for accepting our sufferings."

Across this great democratic experiment called the United States of America, people are wondering what we are becoming. From the time of the Charles Manson murders years ago to the murders of a mother and a group of first graders in a quiet Connecticut town and the in-between growing list, we shake our heads at the senseless violence.

Shaking of heads, tears of sadness and, of course, the expected sensationalistic recounting of the horrors all seem to add up to nothing more than further terror. We can put meaning to a radical religious figure who wants to destroy the nation and understand, at least somewhat, the motives behind his actions. But a young adult who gathers enough high-charged ammunition to annihilate an entire school for no apparent reason? That simply explodes our emotional sensibilities much as a car bomb would explode a vehicle.

From interview to commentary, those with a camera or microphone are testifying on a continuum ranging from the nonsensical ravings of a lunatic to the devouring of a devoutly evil incarnate whose very presence calls for a hyper-vigilance. This undermines our serenity and over-throws the implicit trust in our neighbors. Just as a victim of an unexpected divorce, who upon survival of the shock and the after-shock begins to turn inward, so, too, do all those with even the slightest degree of empathy.

We turn inward to ask ourselves not just who or what the assailant was but, more urgently, what are we becoming as a society. To what degree are we adding to the violence that we are seeing more frequently? How are we promoting peace, justice and the safety of all of our citizens, especially those whose vision has darkened to the point of blindness and whose ears have been closed to the brink of deafness?

Have we become so self-absorbed that we are the blind and deaf ones? Thinking only of "my" as opposed to "our children's" safety and well-being? Are we becoming so voyeuristic from our addiction to reality television's incessant violations of politeness, respect and common courtesy that we don't realize what role models we are becoming for our impressionable little ones?

Even worse, has the political conversation followed suit, adjusting itself from civility and decency to downright verbal assault and public degradation? Is there no longer a place for a once-upon-a-time loyal opposition? Loyal to the rights of all towards life, liberty and the pursuit of happiness?

Many will say that "we" are not to blame: that "he" was crazy, evil and of little or no worth to society. Others will blame his parents and all those who should have seen it coming, who could have stepped out of their comfort zones and gotten him the help he obviously needed. Perhaps even worse, there will be those who will now scream for guns in the hands of teachers. More weapons will be the answer of those who understandably live in fear for their families' safety.

I have shared these and many other emotions. I suppose to be human and fully alive is to be moved to tears and anger. I'd rather experience these feelings any day over becoming so desensitized that I am numb to the goings on of those removed from my daily life. But when I turn inward, as I hope more than a few of us will do, I find myself once again realizing that our national village is mentally ill. We suffer without wanting to name it, but it is real. From depression to anxiety to abuse, we have an elephant in our national living room. And without a strong commitment to face the illness and an even stronger willingness to change our lifestyle, we will become sicker. For all of these illnesses are self-feeding.

Too many of our religious leaders continue to use fear and guilt, passing judgments and enforcing purity laws, all the while living in the shadows of their own rantings. Our political leadership is self-medicating from contracts with lobbyists and the ever-present drive to raise money. Our parents are addicted to surpassing the Joneses rather than simply keeping up with them. All the while, our children are being asked to bear the burden of finding a balance in their lives, what they are interpreting as "be good at everything." And when they come home from this stressful balancing act, they are met by exhausted parents who have self-deported to another space and time, abandoning the children to their own untrained compasses.

Our neighborhoods have all but disappeared, and our gated communities are exceeded only by our gated storage units that poor people pass by in what few buses there are to get them to their second minimum-wage job.

Our schools are crumbling, and our teachers are completely overwhelmed at having to be social workers, parents, disciplinarians, computer wizards and score keepers. Many are poorly trained and even more poorly compensated. Unions have made it nearly impossible to impose stricter standards, while state leaders are fleeing into a voucher system much the same way America fled from integration during the '60s.

Our middle class is dying while the super-rich are dressing up in the grandeur of Marie Antoinette and Caesar, providing sport and cake to keep the masses entertained. The only class that's growing is the working poor; their hopelessness keeps pace. Our children's future is being sacrificed by a national debt that mirrors the family credit card debt, and people sleep at night with the metaphorical Xanax of being able to at least pay the interest.

The nuclear family is a rare species. Fathers in the African-American community are by-and-large absent. Even rarer is a family that welcomes all members to the table equally without qualification or litmus test. We see grandmothers raising grandkids while single mothers are overcrowding the customer service industry, offering a service of scorn and resentment.

The vast industrial complex has overtaken every aspect of our economy, from military to media, and there is only an invisible "they" behind a mask made of the greatest deterrent of all: the threat of nuclear annihilation. Our technology has advanced us so rapidly and so rampantly that we are choking on the amount of information we compulsively shove down our human pipes, not to mention the ongoing distractions and ever-present text beep that invades our focus. It's no coincidence that we have become the "I" world, from iPhones to iPads. The industry makes it all about getting Me-More-Fulfilled when it's really about getting me hooked.

We live for pills more than for fruit, for diagnosis more than for mystery, for getting fixed more than for accepting our sufferings. Convenience has overtaken sacrifice, all manner of chemicals have suffocated sinful and isolation is slowly yet steadily eating away at the cells of intimacy. We are a sick society, and we are in desperate need of a different kind of medicine. Neither the latest pharmacologic discovery nor medical procedure, therapeutic treatment plan or faster airplane can heal our wounds.

Much like those who suffer with Post Traumatic Stress Disorder, we need to slow down, not speed up. We need to sit silently rather than speak incessantly, withhold self-righteousness in favor of patient endurance. We need grounding, positive self-talk and deep breathing exercises. We need to name and face our fears, from the senseless fear of losing our voice in our out-of-control government to the irrational fear of being in the dark. We need mindful processes that help us get through moments when urgency and survival smother our self-control. We need prolonged dialogue of our narratives in diverse populations with the hope that we can learn from each other's shared vulnerability.

Most importantly, we need to put our weapons down, in whatever form they are taking. From guns to words, from tone to passive aggression, from the silent treatment to exclusion, from backbiting to frontal assaults, from religious pontificating to paternal put downs, from shaming to defaming one's character. We need a spiritual conversion, not simply a religious one. We need a community of faith that, despite the violence we see, stands tall against all violence, especially the violence we perpetrate upon ourselves when we consciously or otherwise choose self-destructive behaviors.

It's a prescription that comes not from a position of power

but rather from a position of humility and honesty. Jesus called us to love. Gandhi called us to non-violence. The Buddha called us to enlightenment. Is it now time for us to call our better selves forth and take our society to a higher spiritual level?

As I was coming to completion of my reflection, my doorbell rang. Standing at the door were two women and a small child. They were passing out religious pamphlets. One of the women asked if I would take a few minutes to read it. She was on a mission, and I thanked her for stopping by. She then said, "We are simply asking people if they know the TRUTH, in capital letters."

For an instant, I became resentful, wondering why this woman dared question my knowledge or shame my soul. But then it happened. I looked at the two women and then down at the child who reminded me of the children who were no longer able to walk up to a door. She smiled up at me, and I said softly to the little one, "I know very little. But this I believe: When I have lived a life of justice, humility and charity, I have lived the TRUTH. When I have treated you as the Christ, I have loved the Christ."

I asked them to wait for a moment. Turning toward the kitchen and a warm cake just baked, I wrapped it, took it to the little girl, gave it to her and said, "Merry Christmas." She smiled and hugged my leg. The mother hugged me, and I, without compromise or fear, wrapped my arms around her. For a moment, I felt that those healing arms had perhaps made her feel a little safer in this world of strangers.

A Modern-Day Prayer

"Our mental health has been and continues to be in dialogue with spiritual health, and our attitudes toward life are affected by our childhood religious development."

Growing up in a religious household, I was inundated from an early age with prayers to say on a regular basis. There are many memories of praying the Rosary at least once a week and going to Confession regularly. Memories of making an hour-long, middle-of-the-night devotion to the Blessed Sacrament and of serving as an altar boy to the wonderful priests whom my parents adored.

While the memories are truly a gift in so many ways, I can't help but wonder about the effects of language on such a deeply devoted child with an even more intense religious imagination.

I recall the prayer, "Hail holy queen, hail our life, our sweetness and our hope. To thee do we cry, poor banished children of Eve. To thee do we turn up our sighs, mournings and weepings in this valley of tears. Turn then most graciousness, thine eyes of mercy toward us … that we may be made worthy the promises of Christ."

With as much reverence, I recall being fervent as the prayer continued, "I'm heartily sorry for having offended thee, and I detest the loss of Heaven and the pains of hell, but most of all, because I have offended thee my God, who are't all good and deserving of all my love."

Do I not also remember other prayers with as much vigor? Such as the beautiful Our Father, the prayer to one's Guardian Angel or Prayer of St. Francis? And the answer is simple, in my opinion. Fear takes a much stronger hold on a child's imagination than any other emotion. Therefore, what stuck, more so than the request for daily bread, was the desire for God's will to be done, or the belief that we are guarded by a heavenly force. With that desire came the strong sense of having to be somehow made worthy of that promise.

It is no coincidence that so much of what I hear in my practice is worthlessness, mourning, hopelessness and a sense that each day brings a valley of tears that only a pill, a drink, a gamble, a swindle or a put-down of another can provide. These sentiments are not always coming from people who consider themselves religious. Often, they are from people who have had no religious upbringing or who have left the lessons of their upbringing somewhere along the way.

What strikes me is that regardless of what many profess to believe or disbelieve, our society has been influenced by religious expression. Our mental health has been and continues to be in dialogue with spiritual health, and our attitudes toward life are affected by our childhood religious development. By no means am I concluding that ritual prayers and gestures are detrimental to growth. I am quite certain that with a little research, I could find excellent prayers for children of today. Nor am I concluding that these prayers were detrimental to growth or causal factors of dysfunction.

Nonetheless, I humbly offer to my generational peers the following prayer in the hopes that it will help us continue to flourish both psychologically and spiritually.

> Lord of that which is seen and unseen, creator of my life and giver of free will,

Help me this day to be aware of the limits of my time on this earth that I may use each moment as a responsible steward of my power for good.

Give me confidence in my decisions, in my intuitions, in my God-given life orientation that I may be a model of genuine self-acceptance and humble service.
May I be enriched this and every day, from the first sound to my last breath.
May a little of life's breath be taken away this day, not by the Angel of Death but by the awesomeness of Life.

May I grow this day in serenity, courage and wisdom, Not from being shielded from mountains of sorrow or rivers of pain but strengthened to climb and swim, not with the speed of sound but with the rhythm of love.
Give me courage to walk the paths of life this day boldly, even those difficult and stressful paths, and in so doing, make me resilient and sturdy,
Unyielding to the winds of fear and the temptations of half-truths.
Give me strong shoulders to carry the hardships of this day, determination to face choices with an abiding trust that all results lie in a power greater than self.
Give me both the warmth of blue skies and sunshine to make me smile and the grey skies and clouds to cool my desire for perfection.

May life hold me in its palm, caressing me and my loved ones, giving us not an absence of conflict but the ability to live peacefully within it.
May I remember this and every day that "in the end, all things will be well, and if they are not well, it is not the end."

Amusing Ourselves to Life

"Amusement is undoubtedly one of the great forms of escape from the seriousness of reality. To admit that we are all a bit insane is a pretty healthy admission."

Voltaire said, "The art of medicine consists of keeping the patient amused while nature heals the disease." I've always been fascinated by the phrase, "Humor me for a moment." Cradled in the request may be more than the need for attention. It may, in fact, say something about nature itself and the need to take life much less seriously than we do. We begin, therefore, with The Bathtub Test. How you would score? Take a look, and don't forget to at least smile at the end.

During a visit to the mental health facility, a visitor asked the director what the criterion was which defined whether or not a patient should be institutionalized. "Well," said the director, "we fill up a bathtub. Then we offer a teaspoon, a teacup and a bucket to the patient and ask him or her to empty the bathtub."

"Oh, I understand," said the visitor. "A normal person would use the bucket because it's bigger than the spoon or the teacup."

"No," said the director, "a normal person would pull the plug. Do you want a bed near the window?"

As a mental health professional, I often find myself wishing I had been given a love for number-crunching, engineering or perhaps something in the navigation field. Anything that would keep me grounded in more easily measurable outcomes. But no, I had to be given a love for the mystery of human behavior, the workings of the ever-changing to the never-changing mind. In my work, I get to help clients play "hide-and-go-seek" for their mind and soul, their evolving and sometimes hidden self and their fluid emotions. When I'm lucky, we look for all four at one time.

Such is the nature of mental health work, behavioral change, spiritual discernment, attitude adjustment, self-acceptance or whatever you wish to call it. Those situations that seem to dis-ease us, while certainly treatable with psychotropic drugs, are far more challenging and even inspiring, for they involve developed attitudes, religious imagination, family systems, physical ailments, memories, childhood, adolescence, career, grief, sexuality … the list could go on and on because it always involves the total person.

When I began this work, my sights were set upon helping people find a pathway towards integration, a kind of puzzle-playing. Together, the client and I would pour the pieces of life on a table and work to fit them together towards a beautiful life portrait. Rarely is the path so clear, the puzzle so solvable. In fact, it's often laced with moments of spontaneous amusement that lighten the weight of life.

I recently told someone he was wise. He countered with, "I'm old and wise because I was once young and stupid." I couldn't help but laugh.

When doing a history of the individual, we often ask if there is mental illness in the family. Why, I'm never quite sure, especially since reading a great quote that goes like this: "Insanity doesn't run through my family. Rather, it strolls through, taking its time, getting to know each member personally."

Amusement is undoubtedly one of the great forms of escape from the seriousness of reality. To admit that we are all a bit insane is a pretty healthy admission. When I add a hefty dose of amusement to my day, a safer environment is offered. The pieces have a better chance of fitting together for the individual, and I find that I had very little to do with it, other than providing a safe environment where he or she could accept life as uniquely valuable, even the darkest moments. When I allow a more amusing mood to infect me, I like the ridiculousness of my work and the fact that mystery invades from every corner.

Stepping back, I can laugh at the arrogance with which I sometimes think I can actually help someone find his or her way. The question is, "their way to where?" Can I help people reach their goals and, more importantly, discover what they are? The ultimate goal is death: That's what I want to help people reach? Help people find themselves; and who said they were lost? Help people become more whole; and who said there was anything wrong with being half? Help people feel better? That's a good one. God forbid we should *think* better. Let's just *feel* better.

Happiness is always a better choice than sadness. I would love to know how we reached the conclusion that a blue sky was always more beneficial than a grey one.

Here's another good one: help people change the ones they love. As if either of us has the power to wave our magic wand and actually force change upon the attitudes and/or behaviors of someone else.

If these are not ridiculous enough, I can always help people by enabling victimization. You know, the stuff about blaming everyone else for their problems? That's a good approach, wouldn't you say?

We laugh at these examples and realize how silly they are, yet these are often the puzzle pieces that clients come in search of. Even more silly, I sometimes fall into the trap of thinking such is the pathway to healing. We want instant outcomes, something we can measure, clearly defined right and wrongs, prescriptions that attack the symptoms, concepts that we can think through logically.

This follow-this-course-of-action approach rarely works, however. Because no matter how hard we try, nature has its own pathway to healing and will not succumb to what we call stinkin' thinking, whether a byproduct of alcoholism or some other less-publicized addiction.

Here's the bottom line: When I am sober and serene, I become much more comfortable with accepting life with a humorous attitude, allowing nature to take its course, accepting all that comes my way, fighting less and loving more. When I live with humor as the best medicine, there is much less stress and far more enjoyment of the moment. Yes, even the grey moments. I believe the same can be said for the clients who come to visit with me.

Years ago, when I was suffering from a very deep and seemingly endless depression, life was extremely heavy. But there is a memory that I will never forget. Three months into the depression, I travelled to visit my brother, and sitting at the park, a friend of his cracked a joke. For the first time in three months, I laughed. It was at that moment when I knew the power of resurrection, spring, new life and an awakening of my joy.

Voltaire is probably more correct than I give him credit for.

In the work of mental health, helping people find amusement could be one of the best approaches to take while nature does its job. Looking at the traps I sometimes get caught in trying to cure instead of care, I would do just as well to trust nature as trust the human theories of healing.

But for the sake of those who come here wanting helpful tips, I found these 12 warning signs of good health. (If found in your life, you may rarely need to visit a doctor.)

> 1. Significant growth in network of friends and/or family with whom we feel safe to be ourselves.
> 2. Wider eyes with which to wander to the positive and larger feet with which to walk in the direction of hope.
> 3. Increase in acts of kindness, generosity and gratitude.
> 4. Drive for a greater balance of physical activity, mental exercise and relaxation
> 5. Compulsion to make contributions toward the good of society without compensation.
> 6. Growing tendency to express feelings of affection, tenderness and comfort.
> 7. Increased search for sensitivity toward the needs of self and others, especially those unspoken or residing in the unconscious.
> 8. Ongoing quest for new challenges and expansion of existing expertise.
> 9. Lessening of self-consciousness in social settings.
> 10. More surprise visits from the angel of humor and lightheartedness.
> 11. Further detachment from drama and greater attachment to the ordinary.
> 12. Harboring multiple skills for adapting to ever-changing circumstances.

Positivity and Certainty: Within Reach

"... We can be positive that days will be enriched by a fair day's work; that no harm shall come to those who choose the righteous path, even to the wrath of the strong and self-righteous few; and that keeping it simple keeps the arteries clear."

Two phrases we banter about easily: "I'm positive," and "I'm sure." And yet, we carry an albatross of uncertainty and the weight of negativity.

Being sure is bold. Being positive is not always easy. And so it goes. We utter the words then turn around with the actions. We need to take a break from this ride and reflect on how we've been formed. With a little luck, we just might decide it's time to reset the default. Maybe we have more certainty and positivity than we think.

Take a short break and reflect on the past few hours. What can you say with certainty and be positive about? You'll probably be amazed at all the memories that are neither cause for panic nor reason for jubilation. Most of your memories will be of events, circumstances and experiences that are, for the most part, rather normal, perhaps not even worth mentioning. They are memories of mundane tasks sprinkled with a few moments of laughter. Tasks, conversations, annoyances and anecdotal tales. Nothing of great significance, really, and nothing to be too hyper about. You've been living.

You might be a bit saddened that too much time was invested in the past, in painful memories that you think could happen again. You'll realize it was a waste, and you will smile at the folly of worry over yesterday and tomorrow. In other words, with certainty and positivity, we can say that our lives are, for the most part, regular and routine.

Neurotic movements that intrude on our calmness with voices screaming, "What if…?" might lead us into mud puddles from which we emerge shaking our heads as well as our clothes. We realize that what could happen to us is actually something we are allowing in from the past: We are re-membering, re-playing, re-forming and re-negotiating. We are really dealing with wounds which have not healed, hurts we've not reconciled and attacks we've yet to recover from. In other words, they are like t-shirts that we've bought, worn and outgrown.

What's going on today, once we wade through the mud, is probably pretty normal and sane, at times exciting and at others stressful. We face life with what we possess: our experiences, our expertise, our hopes and our expectations that not only will the sun rise but so, too, will today end. And it does. Such a realization tells us we are capable of attaining a momentous life, a life that keeps us in the moment.

We don't have certainty that we will own tomorrow, but so far, today is going along well for most of us. We can avoid the roller coaster. While we know it sits just across the way, we don't have to ride it until life offers a challenge to grow. Living in the now, we will be able to face that challenge with confidence.

The interesting thing about human nature is that we could be content going in circles; that is, when we stop believing that we're children who are about to fall off. Going in circles is actually the norm. Outlines and rituals are the very stuff of a fulfilled life. It only seems boring to drama addicts who, when all is basically well, immediately wonder when the sky will fall.

Really? Has it ever fallen? For most of us, I doubt it. For all the money spent by advertisers to convince us that it's going to fall if we don't purchase, worry, fight, glorify perceived threats, spend our energy writing scripts or whip ourselves with the belt of guilt, it still hasn't fallen.

It seems to me that two of the best attitudes we can carry in life are certainty and positivity, and carry them now. Not the certainty of a fool or the positivity of a fake. But the certainty that life is worth every breath we take and the positivity that not even life's losses, changes, challenges and destructions can overtake the human spirit.

What can we be certain of? That someone on this planet loves us more than we could ever know. That life is filled with wonder, awe and incredible people. We can be certain that differences in color, sexual orientation, class, knowledge and skill make us a richer nation, and differing personalities do make the merry go round.

We can be certain of a 24-hour day. A smile that a phone call to a friend offers. An angel singing from a hand-written birthday card to a long-lost relative. We can be certain that patience in a long grocery line will influence others to follow suit; that everyone is deserving of dignity; that talking to a problem rather than talking about it will provide a solution; that conflict can be peacefully resolved; and that compassion is equal to competition. We can be certain that greed will attempt to steal away our peace; danger and fear will seek to discourage our dreams; and apathy will make every effort to stop our hearts from beating. We can be positive that days will be enriched by a fair day's work; that no harm shall come to those who choose the righteous path, even to the wrath of the strong and self-righteous few; and that keeping it simple keeps the arteries clear.

We can be positive that for all of the messes we make, it's an everyday miracle that our lives go as smoothly as they do. That we have food to eat, air to breathe, clothes to wear, talents to share. And we can be positive that with just a little effort on our parts, everyone on this planet could have the same.

We can be positive that wars are futile and that poverty is outdated; that the 1 percent are no happier than the 99; that elders are as valuable as grandchildren; that misfits are sometimes more fitting than the fittest; and that darkness can lead us to a brighter light.

We can be positive that being a passenger anywhere on the bus is enough; that neither the front nor the rear offers a better view. We can be positive that gratitude leads to peace, that self-respect leads to serenity and that rest leads to tomorrow's accomplishments. We can be positive that no one has all of the answers, that there is no singular path to truth and that self-confidence, discernment and good judgment are ours for the taking. We can be positive that all we need do is make the next right decision and leave the results to a greater power than ourselves.

Yes, there is certainty. There is positivity. And both are within our reach.

A Priceless Letter

"Indeed, the dividends of hope are far superior to any bank account drawing interest. Would that our attitude toward what we save in life be more reflective of our spiritual values."

I am a member of an extraordinary family. There are eight of us, ranging in age from 45 to 63, who still enjoy the ongoing support of one another. Our parents taught us, particularly our mother, that even in times of stress and emotional negativity, we were brothers and sisters and that nothing was to separate us.

Over the years, we've had our share of crises. In 1993, at the age of 37, I suffered a nervous breakdown and severe depression. My brothers and sisters were there to support me through the darkest days of my life, nourishing me with not only financial support but emotional and spiritual food, the most powerful being unconditional love.

In 1995, my brother Tommy, husband and father of two young children, faced his own mortality when a heart problem led to a pacemaker at the age of 37. Throughout these and other illnesses that have crossed our paths, our mother was always there with her faith and her love. Not until recently, however, did I discover the depth of that faith and the impact it would have on us for generations to come.

Shortly after New Year's, one of my sisters was diagnosed with breast cancer. She would learn a few weeks later that a double mastectomy was necessary. A few days later, I was told after two separate PSAs, there was a one-in-four chance I had prostate cancer. The dreaded "C" word had crashed through the front door of our generation before the New Year's fireworks had fizzled. Like a bandit, it made off with our sense of invulnerability.

When I told people of our conditions and the impending circumstances surrounding them, many called me a pessimist and urged me to think positively, to be strong in faith. "Breast and prostate cancer are the ones you want if you get it," I would hear.

I have always had an aversion to this sort of thinking, mainly because no matter how positive a spin or picture of faith one can frame, mortality still comes knocking. Life is truly very short, and in an instant, we have moved from a free-spirited 19 year old to a 50-year-old manifestation of Alfie's great question, "What's it all about?"

As I continued to wonder as I wandered, I found myself frozen in fear with an impending cloud of doom over my head. That is, until an email message showed up from the "Pace Maker." As the shock of the raid on our health, my sister's in particular, was absorbing our family's inner strength, Tommy slowed down our spiraling pace long enough to reflect upon the strength of our mother's faith that he had received 17 years earlier. He sent us a letter she had written in 1995.

As they had gotten older, both my parents had suffered from several illnesses. My mother had a brain aneurysm, and my father suffered colon/prostate cancer. My mother lived 17 years beyond her prognosis; my father, who suffered cancer at the age of 50 and was given six months to live, is proud to be singing at 85.

With that as background, I pray this letter moves you in whatever way you find worthy of your unique journey through this mortal life. I share it not to convert anyone to

Christianity or to her particular avenue of faith, but because as she aged, she seemed to become almost mystical in her musings about God and life. I also share the letter because I am not only grateful to our mother for writing it but to Tommy for saving it.

Indeed, the dividends of hope are far superior to any bank account drawing interest. Would that our attitude toward what we save in life be more reflective of our spiritual values.

Dear Tommy,

As I sit here reading my Bible, I came across one verse that helped me most of all when me and Dad got sick. I thought you might feel the same as I do and look at life's suffering/sickness differently.

It is one of the great Christian quotations and is found in 2nd Corinthians, Chapter 12, where St. Paul says "WHEN I AM WEAK THEN I AM STRONG." The weaker and older I get Tommy, the stronger I get spiritually. I pray in all things I continue on this path, whatever happens. I use it to praise the Lord of heaven and earth.

I pray you will also use your sickness to make you "better" not worse. Some people become "bitter." I became "Better." I believe you will become "Better" in all you say & do.

JESUS is my best friend, my best Doctor. I can see him more clearly now because he is LOVE. He has opened my eyes to see, my ears to hear, my heart and tongue to proclaim him Lord, King of Kings through his love on earth.

I believe that Jesus will come again and save us from all evil and all sickness. When he comes he will destroy Satan's power. Heaven will then be on earth. Luke chapter 21, v 25.

Tommy, no one has ever seen God, and no one ever will see him because God is "LOVE" and your eyes cannot see. One can only see with the heart. Remember to pray always and in everything you do, and never forget to say "THANK YOU JESUS." You are first in my life no matter what.

Our mother had an 8th grade education.

Creating a Drama-Free Zone
"If low self-esteem is the fuel for relational drama, then the water hydrant must be filled with self-awareness, self-evaluation, self-direction, self-soothing and, ultimately, self-acceptance."

Everywhere I turn, I hear about relational drama. It's either, "I don't do drama," "Too much drama for me," or "She's a drama queen." Not only have I heard it used in melodramatic tones, I've walked into the trap.

For all of its negative connotations, relational drama (RD) is an energy source, a thruster for take-offs and a fuel for many a gossip circle. I have entertained a mix of reactions toward this type of drama, from bothered to bewildered, enhanced by the lack of an agreed-upon understanding.

Like a Sherlock without the luxury of a Watson, I have probed many people for their understanding of RD, and all I manage to extract are illustrations rather than definitions. People can tell when it's going on, but few are able to understand the source or the purpose. Often described as heavy, burdensome, draining, lacking rationale and filled with tragedy, heaves and sighs, RD makes the movie *Imitation of Life* pale in comparison.

There is, however, a common thread that runs throughout every illustration. It has to do with power, or the lack thereof. RD seems to unfold its napkin at the table of insecurity and low self-possession. When people are at a loss – either of self-discipline, self-control or self-direction – those at the table are called like firemen to not only put out their desperate internal fires of self-deprecation, but to give of their own water supply, as well. Not just manifesting insecurity, it seeks to find a source from which to drink, a well that will quench the thirst for safety. RD is steeped in a default fear of a meaningless existence.

RD arises out of one's insecurity with self, limits and acceptance of self. When my life lacks meaning and purpose, I then have to find a way to buffer myself, a way to compensate for my deficiencies. What better way to prop myself up than to bring another person down? What better way to make myself feel better than to make someone else feel worse? What better way to deflect my faults than through the insidious escalation of another's? Such might be a rational behavior if the object of one's gratification needs were not a human being who is being asked to give of his or her life force in order to sustain the insatiable quest.

The antithesis to charity and compassion, RD breeds contempt, resentment, bitterness and guilt. It feeds on escalation of emotion but finds only a partial satisfaction.

Reflect on bullying by kids who believe security is found by taking it from another; schemes by financial wizards who use other people's money to garnish their wages; marriages that "tit for tat" with "you did this" responded by "you did that"; friends who play a game of put downs instead of pull ups; battering husbands whose greatest source of self-regulation is physical abuse; drug addicts who blame the world for their problems and always have a circumstance with which to explain their fall.

RD is a world of take, take and more take. Those who fall prey to it find that with enough practice, a pattern can take root and spread. It's a disease of extraordinary proportion. Our lack of ease (disease), our lack of comfort, our lack of assuredness leads us to do what has been done since the beginning of time. We violate another. We become violent: verbally, emotionally or physically. The tragedy is that we are not seeking a victory in war or even in battle. In the fight itself, we are filled with enough renewed energy until the next shoe comes off. Violence begets violence as RD begets RD.

RD is the result of a perceived lack of oxygen to the soul which leads us to grab the person closest to us and, in that moment of desperation, seek to take a bit of theirs. Even more demeaning to the human person is the awareness that with enough struggle, the person we're seeking oxygen from will start fighting for his or her rights, and the negative emotions escalate.

There is nothing more forceful than an insecure person who knows where to push the button of "you're not good enough" in another and releases a surge of reactions that serve to bolster shame and an atmosphere of toxic fumes that engulfs every participant, creating a web of confusion.

To say that drama can captivate is one thing. To allow one's soul to be captured by relational drama is yet another. For RD feeds on confused interpersonal boundaries by mixing the "I" with the "You." There are no chairs on the stage of relational drama, and people are constantly walking into each other.

This leaves me wondering how can one be freed from the grip of RD? What happens to someone who plants the spear into the ground of his or her existence, who places a chair on the stage of life, sits in it and simply says to the world, "I want to sit in my own chair, thank you very much. I don't want to sit in yours or for you to sit in mine. I want a relational drama-free zone."

Rather than weakening one's power, sitting in one's own chair actually expands it. One begins to be freed. Freed from blaming the world for one's lack of power, from the advertising master that says wearing this perfume will attract hot men, from believing that the new body-building routine will make one more attractive to women, from comparing one's world to another's, from the half-truth that money will create happiness, from thinking that someone else is going provide salvation, from blaming someone for being successful and from relationships that build nothing but fast-moving interstates enclosed by stone walls.

I have learned to sniff out RD in the same way a dog senses the coming of a stranger. Would that I could bark as loudly.

If low self-esteem is the fuel for RD, then the water hydrant must be filled with self-awareness, self-evaluation, self-direction, self-soothing and, ultimately, self-acceptance. Born of flesh and human error but made whole by the ability to move beyond a power struggle, it's been called many names: The Peace of Christ, Serenity, Enlightenment, to name a few.

I call it creating one's own meaning given life's circumstances, playing the hand dealt, becoming self-possessed.

This attitude, while a narrow pathway, leads to peace and helps us navigate through the gift of everyday living rather than script it, direct it, cast it, orchestrate it, star in it or write the reviews. Life is a great play already. There's no need to do any more than enjoy one's own daily show in one's own daily chair. And allowing everyone else to do the same.

A Season for Burning Bridges

"These seasons come, not as enemies but as transformers of our resilience, not as shame-makers of disgust but as rain-makers of grace."

There are seasons in our lives when all that is left is surrender to the unknown; to trust a source beyond all names, definitions and understandings:

> • When all we can do in our desperation is to accept that we must start over, burning self-made bridges that no longer provide security.

> • When we admit that the many and varied love affairs in our lives, either with drugs, work, sex, power, control, victimhood or isolation, are really pain killers that over time lose their ability to provide relief; seasons when we realize that what we assumed to be our closest companions are, in fact, our worst enemies; seasons when we realize that what gave us a few moments of escape from suffering is, in fact, a cruel destruction of human emotion.

> • When we admit to an automatic default to unfairly judge most if not all of authority, be it a boss or a spouse, from the vantage point of a child who continues to feel threatened with abuse, neglect, criticism, blame or abandonment.

> • When we admit to projecting our insecurities onto professional peers as if we were still in elementary school with other children who were protecting their weakness at our expense.

> • When we confess that the demands for success in

our children are not always a validation of their value but rather a puppet show to fill the void of value in ourselves.

• When we accept that we are still unconsciously returning to childhood traumas and the recognition of blocked memories that hurt too much to remember, still associating dusk with teenage returns to home and the memories of sitting on the emotional edge of a tall building overlooking the ocean in fear because parents no longer have the power to save us from having to jump and either sink or swim.

• When we face the memories of the lack of safety in our families when growing up, of heartbreak and betrayal from those adolescent broken loves that people wrote off as puppy, of the shock of friends putting us down in front of others, of the inability to trust our novice sexual feelings with a respected master, of our favorite teacher throwing us under the bus for no reason, of our coach's belittling of us as sissified, of our use of self-degrading humor as a way to get attention, of our staring at walls or sitting in closets, pretending we were somewhere else in order to avoid the war in the next room.

• When there is a desire for something else, anything else, as better than the gods of resentment toward those whose love was inadequate.

• When we repent of hatred toward ourselves for our verbal abuse toward those whom we created to meet our unmeetable need.

These are seasons when at first glance, the coping patterns

chosen to manage the pain seem difficult to imagine as bridges that saved us. They appear as escape hatches from life, and we initially think, "I should have sucked it up."

But under the telescope of the human need for survival as well as the search for divine intervention, we can begin to clarify and even receive these bridges as constructions worthy of our gratitude. For threats against our adequacy, value and esteem, in whatever form or fashion, can also bring forth utter amazement at how resiliently our bridges have been built and how capable we are of creating roads in the wilderness.

Whatever security our bridges from pain may have provided, however, seasons of burning bridges come when we can no longer sustain the fake smile or the phony persona, when the bridges are destroying us and our lives, our families and our careers, our faith and our purpose. These seasons come, not as enemies but as transformers of our resilience, not as shame-makers of disgust but as rain-makers of grace. They come to clean the wounds, soothe with ointment and reapply new bandages. Seasons of renewal come when a knock, which has been there for years, is finally heard, a door is hesitantly opened and an invisible stranger with great powers is allowed entrance into the soul and all of the bridges constructed within; who does not judge or shame the bridges but who gently and with the precision of a brain surgeon helps us speak of the nightmares, admit to the duplicity with which we have lived, leave the secret formulas for coping with pain behind, take off the make-up, stop the hair coloring and let go of the 20s.

The stranger is powerful enough to turn our souls of stone inward to rediscover our inherent worth as souls of flesh; to turn our eyes outward at the same time to see the inherent worth and flesh of even those who have hurt us; to turn our bodies around to face the future; to construct new bridges, transform our limping into walking toward the light and convert the storms of yesteryears into the breezes of new dawns. And, with the wave of a magic wand, create a cosmic spiritual makeover of redemption.

This invisible stranger, once completing the operation, leaves behind not only a request for rest, physical therapy, nutrition and slowly building new bridges but also a prescription for the soul, a spiritual therapy that at first we are told will feel like excruciating pain but which, if daily prayed with others whose season has also come, will gently renew one's strength of character. Building a bridge too valuable to even be appraised, for it is the eternal bridge of life which other seasoned souls will recognize and support.

Spiritual Therapy Exercise

- I have the wisdom to move beyond the limitations of my human mind and worn-out social and religious belief systems into the mind of universal reverence, beginning with myself.

- I have the faith to burn bridges that, though certain, are no longer secure.

- I have a vision of life that tears down the fences of age that no one is too young to learn from, nor am I too old to teach, to meet another goal, dream another dream, fight another injustice, make another friend or shed another tear.

- I have the courage to move into the unfamiliar, accepting life as a laboratory of wonder, showing hospitality to the difference in others and growing indifferent to my fears of change.

• I have a few of the secrets of eternal life: that getting fulfilled is far greater than getting ahead; that the real sign of courage is a gentle whisper for harmony, not an aggressive roar against evil; and that all created things shall pass, even myself.

• I accept that my wants, plans, hopes and dreams that never came and never will can now be wrapped in my old skin that has also been shed and placed reverently in God's bin, and I ask that they be recycled for the good of Mother Earth.

• I dare to believe from this day forward, nightmares can make dreams come true, that darkest nights can bring brighter tomorrows, that trusted anger can create pathways to inner peace and that the bitterness of endings is actually the hopes of beginnings.

• I dare to believe in a spirit of joy, with or without victory, with or without clarity, with or without resolution, with our without pleasure, with or without peace.

• I accept my life and the lives of others, not as outcomes to be projected or a scientific studies to be controlled but, rather, as adventures to be navigated, explorations to be enjoyed, journeys to be embraced and histories that tell of our salvation.

Cuddling with Our Demons

"To spend quality time and speak with kindness to those feelings, emotions and thoughts we so automatically despise in ourselves is to accept aspects that make us all the more human."

It's been said that sometimes we wrestle with our demons; sometimes we cuddle.

We immediately run from the thought of cuddling with our demons. The association with destruction, negativity, the dark side of life, aspects of ourselves that are repugnant and seemingly immoral has an unsettling effect. The word demon comes from "daimon," which means power. So, with a little thought, the daimon is not a bad thing at all. Daimons become demonic when they "overpower" other forces, other powers. In other words, when we become possessed by something/someone, when we become obsessed and can't stop looking at the cell phone waiting for the lover to text, that is "overpowered."

At a seminar with the famous Lou Hillman, I recall a participant asking the following question: "What is going on when someone is obsessed with another? Can't get him or her out of the mind? Can't function or concentrate?" Hillman's answer was curt and short: "When the gods have you, they have you." It may seem that he was trivializing a serious concern. Upon a deeper look, however, his answer was profound and points to the mystery of life and love.

The word infatuation itself breaks down into "false fire." We are caught in the illusion; we literally make something or someone our god and have to be broken down in order to get back to some stability and reason. Thus, it is important to understand that the daimon, or power, is a true gift, but only when used wisely and prudently. And even then, we can't say for sure when we will be overtaken by the "false idols." Having said that, I am led to believe that maybe demons are not all bad. At least the ones I am thinking of.

I used to spend hours wrestling with my loneliness, restlessness, fears of abandonment, anxiety, heartache, self-worth and insecurities. All great powers that longed to overtake my serenity and use up my best energy in the never-ending quest for intimacy. How I spent precious moments wrestling with food, drink and other substances: inner-buddies that in seeking to comfort, turn out to be masked bandits after my soul. Demons are no fun. They can cripple our days and terrorize our nights. They are powerful competitors for our limited energy and call us into the wrestling ring without even the slightest hint of rounds or breaks. We feel as if they have a room full of coaches and trainers, medical personnel ready to heal any wounds they may suffer while at the other side sits a small weakling that makes David look like the giant.

And yet, this is the story we hear and continue to tell. That life is about wrestling with demons. Sometimes we call them issues. And we are convinced that life will not be worth living until they are gone, dissolved, forgotten. I call it a perfection spirituality. Yet it is such a half-truth, such a false account. It's such an unfair judgment; propaganda intended to keep us at war with ourselves. It is little wonder we are always looking for a war as a nation. We can't imagine cuddling with the enemy.

But as Paul Harvey would say, there is a "rest of the story."

We don't have to wrestle with our demons night and day, day and night. And we don't have to run from them through alcohol, opiates, sex, spending or food. We can learn to cuddle with them, at least for a few minutes, and then let them go. To spend quality time and speak with kindness to those feelings, emotions and thoughts we so automatically despise in ourselves is to accept aspects that make us all the more human. These feelings are too often medicated instead of felt.

Many of us have grown up in environments where fear, terror, control and isolated emotions were more prevalent than love and comfort and serenity. Too many have grown up in homes and schools where invisible, 24-hour guards within us kept watch over our safety, ever wondering when the next crisis would come. We may have been physically secure in our neighborhoods, but we were always on alert within our inner homes.

I asked someone recently if she felt she was hard to live with. Without a moment's hesitation, she announced, "Of course I am. I can't imagine how anyone could live with me." I then asked her to think about what she had just concluded. How could anyone live with her if she couldn't live with herself? It didn't take long for her to realize that she had been living a life that was always pointed outwards, while inside, she was longing for self-confidence and self-reliance. She stated that the reason she hated herself was because every time she was alone, she felt lonely, rejected, worthless and needy. I asked her what it would be like if she began to befriend those feelings at night (when they were most exposed) and let them pass through long enough to be cuddled and accepted, then put to sleep along with all of her other emotions.

You see, our world is starving for more affection, more cuddling, more kindness and courtesy, especially to those we say are our enemies. Perhaps we could begin with the enemies within: the ones we dislike because they cause us discomfort and dis-ease. They may not really be our enemies. They are the lost and the broken aspects, the results of trauma and hurt. They are our past inner children that long to be held and comforted. They are the vulnerable and the humbled aspects of ourselves.

I recall a session several years ago with a client, suffering from an opiate addiction, who was talking about everything but himself. In other words, the disease was so powerful it had him on the floor pounding away at his self-esteem by pounding at others. At one point in the diatribe, he looked at me and said, "I'm sure you are looking at me with disgust." To which I responded with complete sincerity, "No, I am so sad for you. I am sad that the disease is eating away at you and that you are exhausted from the fight." He began to sob, and with tears streaming down his face, uttered the words, "I am in such pain, if you only knew."

To some limited degree, I did know, but rather than disrupt his "aloneness," I waited for the next move on his part. He continued to weep. Wondering what was actually triggering the tears, I reflected upon the process up to that point and asked myself inwardly, was the wrestling match with his addiction? Or was the addiction the way he had been treating his sadness and inner pain all of these years?

Is it possible that he was actually wrestling with his sadness and pain instead of cuddling with it? Yes, it's weird, isn't it? To think of cuddling with sadness instead of running from it? Sooner or later, we are, as the saying goes, "running on empty."

I attempted to be as validating as I could, assuring him that he was not disgusting. I wanted to convey compassion, not disgust. He looked at me and, without thinking, stood up and walked over, fell into my arms and cried even more. He needed to be held. He had enough wrestling for the day. It was time to allow someone to be with him in his sadness. To this day, I am convinced he felt that his sadness and pain was the demon he had to wrestle every day of his life. It's little wonder that he self-medicated.

I'm not sure what the outcome was from that session, but I know that he walked out a different man.

"The pain has such a hold over me," he said as he came out of the weeping. "I fought the pain every day with drugs." I asked him if he ever thought of cuddling with the pain, to which he responded, "Why would I do that?"

"Don't you feel a little relief from my holding you rather than scolding you?" I asked.

He cried again and got the point.

I am not advocating that we wallow in our suffering, make love to our traumas or hold on to our past wounds as if they are still open. I am advocating an acceptance of what we seem to find so distasteful: grey skies.

They're just as valid and as real as blue ones.

Reasonable Happiness

"While there is something to be said for the quest towards fullness, there is more to be said for accepting the reality that we pass through this life as stewards, not owners."

I love looking forward to. Anticipation is such a big part of happiness.

I recently looked forward to my good priest friend from Milwaukee spending Easter with me. And it was a step out of ordinary time: an opening of a door that led to a five-day experience rich with sharing of soulful conversation, friendship, prayer and food.

Then it ended. He went back home. We closed the door on the weekend, and life got back to normal.

Today I ask myself the age-old question: What's this rollercoaster ride of life all about? Why do wonderful things, friendships, marriages, great chapters and even great weekends have to come to an end? Why do doors close? Why periods instead of commas? Why is it that we have to come down when we go up?

We say that seeking altered states of consciousness can be an escape from reality. Yet, we seek them anyway: moments when the extraordinary takes over, when we are out of our normal routines, experiencing the joy of the unusual.

Are we to be called unstable for feeling blue after the party's over? For feeling lonely? For wondering why we even bother getting excited about new possibilities when they come to an end?

I recall a therapist once saying to me, "Nicky, when you are on top of the world and all seems to be perfect, when life can't get any better, remember that this, too, shall pass."

So here I am, face to face with life's shortcomings. No matter what we look forward to, nothing in this life will fill the yearning we have for fullness.

There is no person, no drug, no car nor even religious belief that will fulfill our human quest to be in total bliss. Doors open and doors close for us humans.

Yet we continue the quest.

St. Augustine once said, "Our hearts are restless until they rest in Thee." He obviously knew that every quest in his search for the fullness of life left him empty and unsatisfied.

He realized that our hearts cannot be filled in this life, that we will not find total peace and serenity. We will find partial joy, partial understanding, glimpses of happiness and partial fulfillment. We will find havens of rest, moments of rejuvenation, chapters of serenity, but they, too, will come to an end.

We teach our children that injustice is real and that life is sometimes not fair. Perhaps we need to also teach them that we pass through this life forever incomplete. And that no pill, person, job or fifth carport will ease that existential angst.

For students of the Judeo-Christian tradition, we would do well to reflect upon Adam and Eve's desire to become God in eating of the forbidden tree. Such a desire continues to this day. We create our own forbidden trees because we can't help it. We have a propensity toward fullness, and we are restless until we arrive. Remembering God said to Moses of the Jews, which rings true universally, we are a stiff-necked people. We create pathways and idols out of what we believe are "this is it" moments. In our own image, we create the fullness of life, and it falls like a poorly prepared soufflé.

As I sit, accepting that my heart is restless until it rests in Thee, I am allowed to ponder Thee as something beyond anything that this world could offer to me or that I could ever create. And I accept, as did Reinhold Niebuhr in his Serenity Prayer, "this world as it is, not as I would have it. … that I may be reasonably happy in this world and supremely happy in the next."

It's the "reasonably happy" that is the challenge. Those of us who have the time to read, who have ample food, comfortable beds to sleep in and steady jobs to accompany the dawn have more than the 23 percent amongst us who live below the poverty line. That's nearly one in four.

Isn't that reasonable happiness? Isn't such a reality enough to challenge both our propensity and our blues? Enough to move us beyond hunger for the fullness toward helping those who have far less? Beyond disdain for having to come down from a high toward a desire to lift those who are stuck at the bottom?

While there is something to be said for the quest towards fullness, there is more to be said for accepting the reality that we pass through this life as stewards, not owners.

At this juncture of awareness, we are left with the greatest gift of all, the freedom to choose. We can chew on self-pity until swallowed, digested and transformed into bitterness. Or we can spit it out and look to what we have, however partial, as reasonable happiness.

From that vantage point, we can move once again from self-centeredness to service. With this thought, we become less restless and more serene.

On Stings and Things

"I became more aware of my need to cultivate a habit I often shun for fear of being thought of as inadequate. I looked into the mirror and proudly said, 'Yes, I am inadequate, but only in some things.'"

Let's face it. There are times when life stings you on the behind, and all you can do is laugh.

I had just finished recording four podcasts, which took more than three hours of my valuable Sunday afternoon free time, and I was exhausted. I also felt fulfilled through offering a service to those who would be listening and perhaps inspired to reset some of the behavioral default buttons.

With satisfaction, I proceeded to write a Monday Morning Reflection that had been in my head for a few week: *A Dozen Things to Put on in the Morning, Along with Clothes.* As I got to number nine on the list, I received a call from my producer saying there was a glitch in the four submissions and that they would have to be re-recorded. Are you ready to hear what I was suggesting to put on when I received the infuriating call?

#9: Put on an attitude that says, "I, not the circumstances of my life, am in control of my mood."

By now, you are perhaps smiling, thinking that I got stung right where it would cost my credibility the most. It was a bite that would surely test whether I could walk the walk along with talking the talk. I immediately rationalized my declaration of injustice by exempting myself from the commitment. Since it was Sunday, I didn't have to embrace #9. Sunday is a day of rest.

So in my rested mood, I walked outside, screamed at a tree, threw a stick at the fence, cursed the sky and solemnly vowed that my life was a waste and that the gods were against me. I had been so filled with conviction a few short minutes earlier and so empty when the test was placed before me. There I was, sitting still on the ground while asking everyone else to walk the walk. I was so busted!

I rose, not to the occasion, but to use the bathroom. Bladder relieved, I took a deep breath, looked at the bourbon out of my right eye and the chocolate cake out of my left knowing that either would bring relief. But stung again, I realized either choice would also be another way out of self-managing my mood. I looked at the attitude I had just written, gulped from the nasty-tasting but medicinal bottle of self-discipline and lay down on the sofa. In a few short minutes, I thankfully began to laugh at myself and at the power circumstances can have over us. But the laughter was short-lived. The next option appeared. I fantasized about screaming at the producer (just a little). There must be someone to blame. And I am not blaming me.

Half an hour later, after much deep breathing and a few yoga exercises, I decided that screaming at him wasn't the best way to manage my mood, either. I breathed a little longer and a little deeper. When I had calmed myself down, I recalled many times in my life when what appeared to be bad circumstances were, in fact, angels of mercy, preparing me for a better path.

I called my producer and, in an amazingly peaceful voice, said that I would redo them and that first we needed to make sure I had not only set the recorder correctly, but that I also had written down the instructions in detail. And that's when it hit me: I am terrible with details. This was yet another reminder that I needed to take the time to write down directions, instructions and guidelines and not be ashamed.

The moment of awakening. I said with all sincerity, "I probably needed the practice, and the next recordings will be even better. No major loss. All things work for the good of those who believe there is a greater plan than mine. We can't always change the circumstances, but we do have power over our responses. Let's make sure I have the directions clear. I know I can do this."

You may not believe me, but it's true. I not only said it, I meant it. And lest you think I am angry for allowing myself to scream a bit, throw a few sticks, seek out someone to lay the blame upon or even think for a moment that alcohol could help, you're wrong. I observed my feelings and fantasies from a distance and observed my responses like a life coach at a training camp. So grateful that it was Sunday, a day that redefined rest as a period when I didn't have to judge myself or my irrational feelings, I also didn't have to act on them by hurting either myself or another. It gave a whole new meaning to rest. I didn't have to be perfect or even half-perfect. I could rest my "should" and guilt and observe the lower powers without harming anyone.

And from that period of ups and downs, I became more aware of my need to cultivate a habit I often shun for fear of being thought of as inadequate. I looked into the mirror and proudly said, "Yes, I am inadequate, but only in some things." A great teaching moment, huh? I had a chance to firsthand experience how "wonderful life is while feelings (and an observant self) are in the world."

And so, here are a Dozen Things To Put On Each Day (imaginary and otherwise), along with your clothes, of course:

Put on:

12. A bracelet made of Q-tips and remind yourself, from time to time, to Quit Taking It Personally.

11. A stamp on an addressed envelope to a friend you haven't had contact with in a while and write a short note during a break, letting him or her know they live in your memory.

10. A smile after brushing your teeth and have it with you all day long, pulling it out when you meet a frown.

9. An attitude that says, "I, not the circumstances around me, am in control of my mood."

8. A sail and be prepared for the wind's change of direction. We might be going one way and have to change course depending on the winds of life.

7. A positive recorder that automatically stores the significant moments of the day, then reflect on them when the recorder is placed by your bed at night.

6. A tail that wags when you see someone you love, and make sure they experience the joy you feel in their arrival.

5. A sacred bell that rings both when working too hard and when avoiding work.

4. A memory of someone who has died and whom you consider to be an angel looking out for you, invoking their highest spirits to be with you during the day.

3. A mental fan to cool you down the air gets hot, and no, I'm not talking about the humidity.

2. A rope, and tie it to your inner harbor to keep you from floating off into waters of over-personalizing problems.

1. A charger to ensure you always have enough personal power to maintain your integrity and dignity.

And, of course, remember that if you get logged out from not using them often enough, or if you discover that you're not perfect, as did I, simply hit the restart button.

7:17 a.m.

"Everything slowed down, and I moved both intentionally and carefully. I had entered the world of the disabled."

On July 3, 2009, my left retina detached, leaving me the prospect of having only one eye with which to see the world. After four surgeries, hope for restored vision transferred to hope for continued vision in the good eye. While disturbed by the loss, I adapted rather effortlessly to the reality of one eye. Nearly two years later, I awakened on August 10 with what appeared to be minor but nonetheless distorted vision. Thinking that it was time for a new and stronger prescription, I made the appointment and went to see the ophthalmologist the next day.

But the good eye worsened that next morning, and by the time I arrived at the doctor's office, I could not see the paperwork to be filled out. I knew without a doubt my right retina was detaching.

The doctor confirmed my fears and told me that I needed to see a retina specialist immediately. One hour later, I was with the specialist. An hour after that, I was having blood drawn and an EKG performed, preparing for surgery the next day.

August 12 is still a blur, no pun intended. All I remember is that friends and neighbors took over and made sure that I got to where I needed to be and that all of my business appointments were cancelled until further notice. Life had turned yet again on a dime, and adaptation was the name of the game. Survival was the goal.

For nearly two months, I could barely see, wearing the strongest reading glasses available and reading the morning newspaper with both glasses and a magnifying glass. It took well over an hour to read selected articles, so I had to get up at 5 a.m. in order to prepare for work. Everything slowed down, and I moved both intentionally and carefully. I had entered the world of the disabled.

Upon a subsequent visit to the specialist, I was informed that further laser treatment was necessary to provide what he called "insurance." Waiting and reflecting upon life as a disabled person and dependent on the kindness of friends, I learned to live without television, replacing it with music and telephone conversations. Realizing that one of the things so taken for granted, the ability to read, might never be fully restored, I chose to be very discriminating not only with what I read, but on what I would spend the waking hours. As the world sped up, I was slowing down.

I didn't really break down until one morning, when I was standing near the bed, looking at the alarm clock. It was a total blur, and I couldn't see the magnified letters from two feet away. Picking up the clock, I began to cry as I worked my poor vision to make out the time. I cried and I cried, and yet I never asked, "Why me?" I just wept, feeling the loss and asking for God's help through this latest gift.

What could I learn? How could I change? In what ways would I become a better, more compassionate human being? What was life's lesson in this latest classroom?

How could I utilize the advances in technology to assist me and allow me to live an even fuller life. For truly, one can have the greatest vision in the world and not see. Which is why I asked for insight, a different way of seeing. During my stint with blindness, I asked for a vision of acceptance, gratitude, understanding, patience, empathy and courage.

On Tuesday, October 4, I was told the oil could be taken out. Hopefully, the retina had not only attached, but the laser had added a protective shield. I smiled, thinking if only life were as simple as putting up shields to protect us from harm. But the starship *Enterprise* I am not.

By late afternoon, the oil was out, and I was home after the sixth time on the surgical table (each surgery had a second one, at which time the oil was taken out). I came home crying yet again, mainly from the joy that hope was still alive. The doctor had given me a good prognosis and said that in a few days, I should have restored vision, perhaps not 20/20, but certainly close.

Apparently, I didn't hear "the few days" part and went home despairing that I still could not see. The next day I awoke, and again, the alarm clock was blurry. I continued to use the drops as prescribed and got a ride to work as usual, barely able to see. I began to doubt my ability to recover as well as the assurances of the doctor. That night, I went to bed, seeing a bit better but still not at all clearly. There sat the alarm clock, and here sat a nearly blind man who could not tell time without a magnifying glass.

Waking up my usual 5 a.m., I got up, put on a robe and proceeded to get a cup of coffee. I had given up on reading the paper. I sat for a couple of hours in meditation, reflecting on all the great Broadway shows I had seen, the many cities I had experienced, the great buildings I had walked through, the magnificence of natural wonders such as the Grand Canyon.

Upon returning to the bedroom to get showered, it happened. I looked at the alarm clock across the room and dropped my coffee. There it was: 7:17 a.m. I could see.

I fell to my knees and wept, this time for joy. My vision had returned almost overnight. The doctor was correct: "In a few days, I would see much better." Never in my life will I forget that time: It is etched on my heart, in my mind and, even more so, within my eyes.

Never again in my life will I take anything for granted, including the loss of sight, for even that can be a blessing. I am still moving slower and more intentionally, still reading what matters, still watching very little television, still enjoying the resetting of life's default through this latest chapter of my life.

All that I ask of those who are able to read this article is this: Every morning for the next month, or for the rest of your life, stop at 7:17 a.m. and be grateful for your vision. And pray that you not only see with your physical eyes but with your spiritual eyes, as well.

Sometimes I Sits and I Thinks ...

> *"Some would have us believe that letting the world pass us by is counter-productive and a waste of precious time. I say such an attitude is rooted in our Type-A culture and that we desperately need to simply sits and shift down."*

Years ago, my father gave me a handmade wooden plaque with the following quote: Sometimes I sits and I thinks, and sometimes I just sits.

The gift has traveled with me for the past 28 years, but only recently have I more deeply appreciated the significance.

For many years, I yearned for a period during the day when my mind would simply take a recess and stop moving. It was as if I yearned for red lights, roadblocks, traffic jams: anything that would bring my spinning mind with its array of thoughts, ideas, fantasies, dreams, nightmares, stresses and worries to a screeching halt.

The more I worked at what I had learned would be the path to perfect union with the Divine – to simply sit without thoughts – the more I found myself thinking!

Sorry, Mr. Buddha, this detachment thing just doesn't work for me the way it may have worked for you.

I can't shake the reality that when someone tells me to *not* think, that's when I automatically think. It finally hit me that the problem wasn't with the wisdom of the quote; the obstacle was found in my ego. All I needed to do was let go, literally, of all thoughts and simply let them be, let them pass through me without my attention, to stop holding on to them as if they were the Grail, Holy or Unholy.

Watch yourself sometime when you don't respond or react to something that comes your way, and notice how, most of the time, what could have been an escalating event, either positive or negative, just vanishes into thin air. I'm sure that's why sages often remind us to put most reactions that seem so urgent off until tomorrow; and when tomorrow arrives, we will ask ourselves, what was the rush?

To just "sits" means to disregard the thoughts (especially the self-defeating ones), devalue their importance, window shop the interior world without buying, resist the urge to enter into a dialogue with the thoughts, allow the mind to just flow like a babbling brook, with neither engagement nor judgment. The babbling is simply that. Babbling. And there is no reason, during the "sits" time, to give it any more leverage over one's soul than it deserves. In fact, babbling in and of itself, without analysis or shame, is truly calming to the soul and allows us to simply sit and watch life pass by.

When we sit back, away from the interaction with the mind, we are giving space between ourselves and a larger power: the power of space where the divine Mr. or Mrs. Clean can work his or her magic and cleanse the cracks of our lives. And that's the paradox. When we just sits, we are provided a pathway to becoming more productive when the mind is put back in gear.

Some would have us believe that letting the world pass us by is counter-productive and a waste of precious time. I say such an attitude is rooted in our Type-A culture and that we desperately need to simply sits and shift down. In fact, I have always believed that the productivity of a classroom is inextricably linked to not only physical activity, but also to time outs, recesses and unstructured play.

To sits is not about shutting down the mind. It is about allowing the mind (imagine a car's engine) to sit idle, still running but sitting in neutral with the brake on. And just as with an automobile, when the mind is in neutral and the brake is on, it's going nowhere. And we, the drivers, are safe to simply "be" for a few minutes.

I recall in great detail being a child getting ready for school in the middle of winter and looking so forward to getting in a heated auto in the early morning frost. My father, one of the most thoughtful men I've known, would go outside 10 minutes before leaving for school, turn on the engine and just let it run. He would walk back in for the last couple of minutes of *The Three Stooges* and wait for the car to do its thing. When the engine had warmed up, he would go out to turn the heat on and signal to us that the car was ready.

Perhaps that act by my father wasn't much, but it was a tender reminder of how important it is to let our minds run a little in the morning, but not in gear. In idle. No offense to the Great Religious Prayers, but frankly we've spent entirely too much time on rote prayer and invocation in our religious culture and far too little on simply being in the Presence without doing or even saying anything. I call it mind piddling.

Trust me. There are few exercises for one's mental health greater than just sitting and letting the mind flow without reacting to the thoughts or letting them overtake us.

And the more we practice this simple and powerful form of meditation, the less we will react to the endless array of stimuli in our chasing-after-our-tail world.

Bullying: Uncovering the Cause

"Bullying is actually too soft a word for what the behaviors truly are. Any form of bullying, from impugning one's character to silencing one's voice, violates the human spirit."

Tim Fields said, "While accidents and assaults kill people quickly and spectacularly, bullying and consequent prolonged negative stress kill people slowly and secretively. The outcome, though, is the same."

Bullying is on the rise, so much so that we have a category of assault called Bullycide. A growing topic of national conversation, bullying is more complicated than the casual talking points we hear and much wider spread than just the playgrounds, locker rooms and middle schools. As someone who was bullied, I've reflected on this societal sickness and reached some rather disturbing conclusions.

In the beginning, bullying may be an experiment to discover Mr. Hyde. In the end, it is nothing more than a beastly and cowardly pattern of violence.

Bullies are neither self-assured nor strong. They are but well-disguised weaklings masking their own fears and shortcomings. Sadly, underneath that mask is, according to Macbeth, a "poor player who struts and frets … full of sound and fury, signifying nothing." Behind the curtain stands a coward.

Bullying is a ritualized and well-designed program of cruelty that finds the tender among us and invisibly thrusts a knife into the core of his or her self-worth. Ironically, with each jab, an internal stab poisons the empty soul of the bully. Manipulative, mean-spirited and contemptible behavior, bullying wounds both victim and bully and, while publicly condemned, often continues to be minimized as part of the socialization process. The repeated physical or non-physical, verbal or non-verbal Cowardly Putting Another Down Syndrome is a language rapidly spreading. From where it originates, I cannot conclude, but how it is passed along is clear. Bullying is not passed along through the acts of children; more alarmingly, it's through the behaviors of adults.

From sexual harassment to economic disparities, from exclusion of co-workers to picking away at a wife's self-esteem, from gossip among neighbors to lobbyists who threaten politicians, abuse of perceived power is to adults what bullying is to children. Without making a blanket statement about all adults, let's face the facts.

Cowardly bullying is occurring in workplaces by authority figures as well as in classrooms by teachers. It can be found in rental properties as well as school cafeterias, political landscapes as well as girls-night-out parties, assisted-living facilities and even football fields. On domestic fronts as well as on school buses, religious organizations as well as soccer fields, conference rooms as well as faculty lounges, the liberal press as well as conservative schools are not immune from this infectious self-destruction.

Bullying is not merely a one-on-one or small-group problem. It is happening on a corporate, calculatedly threatening basis that simply says, "Play by my rules, or you're out," and even more viciously, "Play by my rules, and you're out anyway." For when humans are seen as commodities, there is always a replacement waiting to be bought.

Bullying is actually too soft a word for what the behaviors truly are. Any form of bullying, from impugning one's character to silencing one's voice, violates the human spirit.

Bullies are no less than predators that prey upon and seek to devour the vulnerable. Whether overtly directed or passively understated, the world of bullying strikes out with aggressive, blaming and morally judgmental attitudes. It assaults with highly strategic agendas that stigmatize and victimize targeted persons and groups for no other reason than to humiliate, offend and dehumanize. These behaviors are not only "put downs" in order to "build up" the bully. They are acts of wannabe emperors who underneath delusions of grandeur are nothing more than cowards who feed on trampling.

Some would call it survival of the fittest. I call it a grave and mortal sin against the dignity of the human person. Discrimination against age, sexual orientation, wealth, educational level, religious affiliation, appearance – these are all attitudes that need to be challenged for what they are often rooted in: cowardly bullying. The sad fact that parents are more interested in fixing their children's teeth than caring for their inherent dignity is more tragic than any of Shakespeare's works.

The sadder fact that siblings, best friends, colleagues and relatives speak and act in repeated and enduring aggressive ways toward each other, habits so ingrained that the pain inflicted is regarded as "the way we relate," serves to prove how desensitized we are becoming.

Marital discord is all too often the bi-product of a well-developed form of mutual bullying, with each partner having perfected both an attack mode and a line of defense.

And the escalated stepping on each other, through either withdrawal or verbal attack, whether poking at the tender areas of one's hurts and traumatic memories or looking for stress points to exploit, leads to what becomes the expected and even "comfortable" outcome. Comfortable because the power of bullying lies in repetition and association. As creatures of habit, we shape our very identity around what we all know to be "the mother of all learning." Therein lie the impenetrable powers of bullying. Just as bullying plunges a knife into another's self-esteem, without the bully, one can learn to feel even more powerless.

The great human dilemma is that there is safety in what we've come to know and expect, even when it is an abusive expectation. We are hardwired for a center of the universe from which to read the world, and bullies begin to serve the Master Bully at an early age as both destroyers of our natural centers and creators of our "learned" centers. So the starving learn to bow before dictators, children learn to expect being tripped, middle-school students learn to expect a behind-the-back-attack, couples learn to interrupt each other with disdain, husbands expect below-the-knee hits from old doors yet to be closed, colleagues learn to sub-group and talk about the perceived misfits, mystics expect religions to exclude and isolate them. Citizens expect to be terrorized by fear-mongering politicians, and viewers expect media stars to burn down competitive channels with verbal lighter fluid. Habitual consumers that we are, we steadily buy into what we think is security when what we get is a tighter rope around our necks.

It takes great courage to choose freedom over security, justice over the status quo, activism over mediocrity, fairness over size, mystery over knowledge. It takes even greater courage to admit that bullying will always win when we avoid involvement by giving ourselves a false sense of peace that it's "him/her/them and, thank God, not me/us." An incomplete sentence but not thought, the missing word is YET. "Not us, yet."

Perhaps our hope lies in confessing that we have fed the wild and starved the tame, awarded the winner at all costs and blamed the weak for all problems. Perhaps we can awaken to the reality that we have succumbed to the power of the fake Oz and ignored the power we already wear. Perhaps we can fake it 'til we make it, pretending that we have accidentally broken the cane of false security and found ourselves still standing. Such are the first steps toward a conversion of hearts.)

Bullying: Love is the Answer

"This higher power gives us strength to defend the voiceless and stand against all oppression. It provides the courage to resist categorizing some of God's children as somehow better than others."

A recent conversation with a colleague led to the question, why? With all of our advances, with our emphasis on self-esteem, our knowledge and socialization skills, why is bullying becoming more prevalent?

The answer may be oversimplified, but it seems that the more we have materialistically, the more we lack in self-worth.

Over the decades, we have become increasingly viewed as human buyings rather than human beings. We're bought and sold, traded like things no less often than our iPhones are traded for the newest version. We've replaced shoe polish with new shoes, crow's feet with botox, outdoor socialization with electronic games. We've also replaced long-term goals with instant access, tellers with ATMs and cashiers with computer check-outs. The world of me has now become the world of E: from E-bates to E-zine, from E-bay to E-cigarettes.

Our human values have been challenged, and we are unconsciously fighting for our worth as our spirits feel less and less valuable. Scarcity of jobs, rise of school tuition, decline of America's greatness, increasing competition for grades, rise in crime, overload of extracurricular activities, constant reinventing of social hierarchies and name-calling political discourse: With these realities slamming against us each and every day, there is little wonder that the future leaders of our nation are fighting each other and laying claim to whatever turf they can find to call their own.

Even with all of our advances, we continue to sink in the quicksand of the primitive brain, believing that if there is scarcity, either of love, validation, supervision, worth or education, then there must be a way to compensate. Consequently, there must be a group or a person who provides compensation.

There is simply no way to stop bullying without a national conversion, a choice to turn hearts of stone into hearts of flesh. A renewed commitment to restore our families, schools, workplaces, grocery stores, political discourse, neighborhoods and public conversations to human decency. Notice I said "restore," not "return to."

We are living in a much more sophisticated and scientific age. The days of Ozzie and Harriet are long gone, and living out family values is a far more nuanced task than some traditionalists would have us believe. We can no longer walk around drunk on nostalgia, materialism or ignorance. We can no longer pretend that excluding and avoiding those who are deemed impure, particularly the poor, addicted, homeless, jobless, uneducated, different, unskilled and unloved, is the answer. We have seen that "moving away from" costs us more in the long run. Only in accepting our own addictions, facing our fears and seeing the commonality of our slavery to the Master Bully will we become more enlightened and aware when bullying is raising its terrorizing sword, taking it down with courage and love.

Such awareness comes when we resist the urge to become human buyings and resist viewing others as such. It comes when we choose socialization, accomplishment and the supervision of our children over giving material things and doing their homework for them. When we urge the care of shoes and the value of crow's feet; when we see wisdom in the old and hope in the young; when we become more empathic, compassionate and less drawn to survival of the fittest, richest, smartest. When we value our children more than our three-car garages. When we promote the choice of a diversity of friends. When we reject all forms of violence.

Only through acceptance of our powerlessness will we find a higher power to restore us to sanity, bringing forth a day when the words bully and victim will disappear from the face of the nation.

The very reaching for a power greater than ourselves provides a medicinal balm for the emotional pain, life's storms and wrecks, human weaknesses of heart and mind. It surrenders, not to the senses, but to the senseless, to mystery, to what is seen only by faith, to "the 8th day, when every tear will be wiped away."

This higher power, which I call Love, gives us strength to defend the voiceless and stand against all oppression. It provides the courage to resist categorizing some of God's children as somehow better than others. It gives us eyes of wonder and hearts of openness. It is a fundamental societal shift that transcends all religious doctrine and renews the world.

As a result of our recovery, our interventions will be about building. If bullying is passed through adults, then we as adults must embrace behaviors, responses and options that promote the higher power within us, encouragement towards teamwork, achievement, empathy, compassion, service, active listening, understanding and even validating one's fears as well as hopes. One can't simply stop bullying by saying "stop." The only true interventions are those that believe in and draw forth one's higher and truer self. It is a systematic reprogramming, wiping the dust off of our birthrights as equal participants in our search for life, liberty and the pursuit of happiness.

We can slowly eradicate bullying one event, one confrontation, one intervention at a time, challenging ourselves when we are tempted toward these behaviors:

- Nit-picking, fault-finding and trivial criticism
- Half-truths to distort someone's character
- Undermining one who is not present to defend himself
- Entitlement to any "wants" that can easily be lived without
- Attitudes of self-righteousness and discrimination toward those who are different
- Name calling of any sort
- Singling out and treating people differently
- Marginalizing, overruling, ignoring, sidelining, freezing out
- Belittling, demeaning and patronizing, especially in front of others
- Replacing the human person with automation without training in another area of need
- Humiliating, shouting, threatening, tripping or name calling often in front of others
- Overloading with work
- Increasing responsibilities without adequate pay-raise equity
- Refusal of annual and sick leave
- Denial of training necessary to fulfill one's duties
- Making a job unbearable so the employee will

eventually quit
- Distorting and misrepresenting things said by others
- Coercing someone into leaving through no fault of their own
- Seeking the inner circle to the exclusion of others
- Disallowing and disavowing interracial love
- Creating anticipated terror in another
- Cyber and text messaging hatred, ridicule and attack
- Dehumanizing another through blame
- Using authority and power to threaten and manipulate
- Affording children less dignity simply because they are vulnerable.

We can admit our powerlessness over materialism and claim a power greater. We can restart our internal engines this day, fueling our mind with the courage to live in search of truth, oiling our tongues with the milk of kindness, tuning our decision-making skills with the strength of conviction, filling our shoes with the warmth compassion and empathy and caring for others justly and tenderly. And we can renew the face of the earth, not with botox, but with Love.

From Too Much to Not Enough: Time to Empty the Trash

"It's a world of opposites that has taken over our souls, leading our neurosis to Xanax to ease our anxiety, opiates to fuel our normalcy and pornography to induce a moment's pleasure. The poor have crack while the rich have Loratab."

How often we hear the phrase, "I've got too much on my plate."

And yet, buffets are popping up everywhere, from s uburban shopping malls to interstate exits. All You Can Eat has overtaken Fine Dining. Bombarded with options, from thousands of apps to the over-abundance of On-Demand, we've become spiritually bipolar, swinging from seeking limitless pleasure on one hand to self-deprivation on the other. We feed our desire to play God while starving our need to be human.

Rather than honor the loneliness and emptiness that comes with being human, we become super-human doings. Our inner hero wears an iron mask that instead of protecting us, weighs us down. We're more overweight than ever before, super-sized and ever expanding. We're building storage units on every corner, and hoarding has become a reality TV show that has thousands of viewers, or, I should say, gawkers. All the while, we're under-nourished, sleep-deprived, socially underdeveloped and starving for intimacy.

We deprive our underprivileged the basic needs of reading and writing. Yet, we amass stockpiles of homes, from snowbird to summer, villas to cabins. We enslave ourselves within gated communities to keep people out, all the while being desperate for community. We interface with anonymous, faceless personas in chat rooms, becoming so obsessed that nights pass like minutes while genuine life purpose starves for attention. We distrust those we work with on a daily basis and enslave our hearts to encounters with strangers as we look for the fulfilling Match.com.

We don't need an invasion of body snatchers. They're already here, eating our way to total discomfort and moving on up the ladder of workaholism that everyone but us knows to be a downward spiral. It's a world of opposites that has taken over our souls, leading our neurosis to Xanax to ease our anxiety, opiates to fuel our normalcy and pornography to induce a moment's pleasure. The poor have crack while the rich have Loratab. And both are pathways to suicide.

Anti-depressants have become as common as vitamins, and there's always alcohol which, if challenged as addictive, would receive a resounding chorus of cease and desist. God forbid we should go through the pain of withdrawal from anything. We've become so drugged that we now have methods of reducing our substance abuse through the addition of substances that not only block the urge for other substances, but block any withdrawal.

Even in religious circles, we are seduced into adding. I am stunned at how often we hear prayers to "fill us with," to "give us more." We are possessed by a need to be filled with whatever is the spirit of the moment. Rarely do we hear prayers (except occasionally during the season of Lent) that ask for us to be emptied, to be stripped, to be laid bare, to be naked before the living God. It's as if our human shame leads us from not being fully clothed to being overly stuffed. Look in our closets, and count the items of clothing that we need and yet never wear. Check to see how many freezers we have or how many unnecessary piles of junk lie in drawers. Forever saying it's time to empty out, they just keep accumulating until by the grace of God and perhaps the aid of Adderall, we organize and discard. But rare are these moments.

It's little wonder we are always on edge. We move from having too much on our plate to adding more and more. And when we say "no" to a request, we feel compelled to give an explanation, as if a simple "no" is not good enough, not satisfactory to our need to feel loveable. Saying "no" is just too hard. Saying "no" risks the threat of anger and bridges burned. And so it becomes a "scratching of each other's back" rather than a self-awareness that sets healthy boundaries.

Over the years, when I've asked people to make changes in their lives, they immediately assume it means to add a behavior or attitude. Rarely does anyone want to hear that there are two keys to mental health: One is replacing a behavior or attitude. The other, and far more challenging, is emptying the behavior and simply being without. Ask any alcoholic, and he will tell you it's easier to smoke a cigarette and drink coffee at a 12-step meeting than to just sit and feel the pain of not having a fix.

I have a great quote hanging in my office that reads, "The happy person is not the one who has the most but the one who needs the least."

In a society that focuses on needs and wants (remember the addict's favorite line is, "I want what I want when I want it, and I want it now."), it would do us all well to move from a childish way of thinking to a more adult way. This is a challenging task, to say the least.

Not long ago, I was grocery shopping with my niece and nephew. As we walked each aisle looking to fill the list of necessities, they both found something on each aisle they wanted. Calmly and serenely, I said, "It's just the urgency of the moment." While thinking I was the nutty shrink uncle, they nonetheless experienced the frustration and moved on.

When we approached the checkout lane, I glanced to the left and saw a slice of heaven: a Starbucks coffee stand toward which I began making my way, telling my niece and nephew that I would be right back. They were to watch the cart. No sooner had I moved away did they grab my arm and, with the same serenity, say, "It's alright, Uncle Nicky. It's just the urgency of the moment." I had been busted. We laughed and discussed how controlling the urgencies of life is a lifelong journey.

If we adults could be comfortable fighting our urges for more, for the moment to be filled, if we could learn to not only teach delayed gratification but live within its walls, we could change the face of this society and live with less, creating a climate where there is plenty for all. One might call that the redistribution of wealth. Hogwash, I say.

Sharing a coat when there are 10 hanging in the closet is the quintessence of Christian Charity. And emptying one's cupboards, closets, storage centers and shelves might help us realize that happiness really does reside in those who need the least. Remember, emptying closets doesn't mean refilling them.

There are two pathways: When we have released our higher

selves, we usually get to the halfway line and replace. Perhaps we can hit the highest self this year and score a touchdown by simply being without.

It's a different kind of prayer. Rather than asking to be filled, we ask to be emptied. In my religious tradition, it's called fasting. Not a bad idea for both spiritual and mental health.

In fact, if we empty ourselves of some of our baggage, including prejudices, resentments, bitterness, superiority and inferiority complexes, to mention but a few, it might give a whole new meaning to being fulfilled.

Fouls, Flags and Playing within the Guidelines of Life

"... no personal, emotional, spiritual or physical boundaries can be respected, much less maintained, without an assumption of reverence for the human person."

Whether it's basketball, football or baseball, there are boundaries. There are fouls and there are flags, whistles and markers. Everyday life is also a game, a sport of its own design, and just as with any other sport, the game of life has boundaries and rules, flags and fouls.

The personal boundaries of life are different because they take place on the ever-changing turf and courts of the world. We know not by whom, how or when personal boundaries will need to be arranged and rearranged because in life, there are too many variables, too many mysteries, too many surprises, all of which make it all the more exciting.

While I am not sure how to give tips for setting boundaries, I can say with a certain amount of confidence that no personal, emotional, spiritual or physical boundaries can be respected, much less maintained, without an assumption of reverence for the human person. And so I offer a few guidelines for setting boundaries, for making judgments about them and for realizing that in the game of life, there is no instant replay. Give it your best shot, and live with those who will question your call, believing that you are your own best coach, player and referee. You are Three in One.

1. Revere yourself, despite your history, mistakes, losses sure up to others. You deserve to be treated with dignity, reverence and, above all, validation. In other words, each

of us has legitimacy. We don't have to explain or justify our existence and inalienable right to pursue happiness. No one has the right to treat you as if you are second class, damaged goods or commodities for their vain glory. Let no one mistreat or discredit your goodness, despite behaviors that you may engage in that go against your dignity and devalue your own worth. Instead, learn from self-abuse and the dishonor of others. Reset your compass to point in the direction of valuing human life.

2. Revere fairness and justice in all of your dealings. When overstepping and invading the dignity of another, apologize immediately, and then drop it. When you feel someone has hurt you or your pride, step up and call foul and then move on without bitterness or revenge. When someone you know is being degraded or judged without proper defense or rebuttal in your presence and not available to defend themselves, call for a cease and desist immediately and bring the conversation back to those in the here and now. When conflicts arise between "goods," which is most often the case, discern the greater good for the moment, sacrificing one's turf when necessary and always seek the common good.

3. Revere your needs and preferences as well as those of others. Be acutely aware of your personal rights: the rights to your feelings, privacy, opinions, perceptions, values, thought processes, needs and preferences, even pain and adversity. Be aware that those around you deserve no less reverence.

4. Revere your propensity for selfishness. Be even more attuned to your wants and your defenses, your selfish instincts that seek survival at all costs. Be aware of their power, and rather than judge the voice of the survival brain,

which automatically moves toward flight or fight, respect it and tame it with love and care. Knowing that wants at the expense of others and defensiveness from harm, while understood to be protective, are more often destructive to the inner world of emotional health. Discern the difference between urges that are fed by "I want what I want when I want it" as well as walls of fear and shame that seek to isolate and starve the human need for intimacy from those impulses that come from years of wisdom and insight and which always serve to better the world. Be aware that urges in and of themselves are not evil, but many defensive urges were formed long ago when we were powerless over our environments and sought respite from the cold of terror. Believe that even these urges long to be rechanneled for good.

5. Revere your intuition and ability to discern. Be ever vigilant toward those with whom you do not feel safe emotionally. Be cautiously guarded with those whom you are unsure of, and be at ease with those for whom you feel an implicit trust that their intentions are honorable.

6. Revere others, especially those whom you dislike, and look deep within to find the part of you that they emote. Be gentle with those dark sides, knowing that you, too, harbor the potential within. Be a safe harbor for those with whom you share life and work, that they may disclose their worlds with authenticity. Seek the best in others, and yearn to bring it forth, respecting each one's journey as a precious tapestry in the making.

7. Revere the ebb and flow of intimacy and separateness. At times we will feel close, and at other times, we will feel distant from even our closest companions. This is natural and needs to be accepted as a part of growth.

8. Revere the process. All too often, when boundaries are invaded, when you are unclear where you end and another begins, when the enmeshment is so intertwined that blame no longer works and there is literally nowhere else to go, such is the time to sit with the uncertainty and trust the process, to let go of the need to perform surgery on each other or find resolution. It could be the greatest statement of trust in something larger and a chance to wait patiently together, letting time work its magic. Be careful of the adage, "Don't let the sun go down on your anger." Perhaps it need be expanded. Perhaps the sun going down is too literal. Perhaps a greater call is to love, even when we are angry, to be with someone whom at the moment we don't want to be with, to trust that there will be a dawning of a new day, a new way, a new opportunity for resolution. Sometimes, we get too fixated on resolving everything on our chronological "sun down" and forget that God may live in a different time zone.

9. Revere the uncertainty of life's easy answers, and live with an appreciation for mystery, withholding judgments from those who seem to make it so easy. Remember the famous song from *Porgy and Bess* that so wonderfully states, "It ain't necessarily so." Be careful with judgments as to who's worthy and who's not, who's on our side and who's not, who's victim and who's perpetrator. Be careful with judgments about the identified sick person within the family and whether the sickness may well be in the system. Be aware of the more healthy: he who admits to making mistakes or he who denies any or all culpability. Be careful regarding the one to worry about most: the quiet and shy one who never questions authority or the defiant one who is determined to make his or her way. As we have learned over the years, life is not always what it seems; nor are people and events. I'll never forget a line someone shared

with me years ago: "Even Judas had a mother." I also remember a mother telling me she had one daughter who was perfect and another who was Satan in disguise with all of her defiance and struggle for power. I shivered as I responded, "I'm more concerned about the perfect one."

10. Revere the foul, the mistake, the flag, the breach of faith, the failure, even the sin. Revere that we are human and that we cannot grow without having to face our faults and our flaws, our propensity for corruption. Mistakes, flaws, faults, limitations, imperfections – these don't make us unavailable or unable to love. Rather, they are the very pathways to love. We walk with each other, and from time to time, we ask those we love to be our walking cane, our rocking chair, our angel of mercy. We need their wings on which to fly and their ointment with which to heal. The tragedy of today's political, corporate and even parental scene is that we don't hear enough apology; we don't hear enough admission that humans make decisions, which means we will screw up sometimes and have to go back to the lab of life and try again. Given the choice, I'd take my human mistakes and failures any day over becoming a robot, as long as I have a laboratory to keep going back to and friends with whom to keep growing.

The Voice of Abiding Love

"Accepting fear is respecting that which is greater than human achievement. Accepting fear is reverencing a power greater than what we have come to know."

The voice of darkness would have us believe that we are used goods, second rate and tarnished; that in our essence, selfishness and sadness unto death are our lot.

The voice of death would have us believe we are destined to be consumed and then thrown away, of little use beyond the momentary glitter that soon fades.

And so we avoid listening to ourselves for fear of what we will hear: a shrilled siren of mistakes and errors.

The Voice of Abiding Love tells a different story and provides a glorious ending.

The Voice of Abiding Love is the voice most capable of providing the intimacy we long for, the serenity we crave. By releasing us from both longing and craving, the Voice of Abiding Love breaks down the defenses of the ego and offers the gift of lasting peace.

This Voice of Abiding Love is born in the stable of one's internal home, in a place where few would lay their heads much less search for inner peace.

The Voice of Abiding Love is born in self-acceptance. And what is self-acceptance? It is the embracing of the most highly developed aspect of ourselves: our need to control life. This need, which is capable of neither fulfillment nor satisfaction and which ultimately leads to self-loathing, cries out for a welcoming home.

Self-acceptance is opening the soul's door and showing genuine hospitality to the need for control, believing that in our formative years, this seemingly unrelenting enemy was once our protector and our friend. Self-acceptance is to repent, to literally turn control around to see it for what it truly is: a broken attempt at heroism. Not so long ago, as delicate children, we had to succumb to the crippling paradox of humanity. We came to a crossroads early on and chose the false pathway to peace. Although we believed that in order to be saved, we must die to self, we defied the notion of surrender and chose that of suicide. We would kill ourselves before we would surrender to the unknown. Why? Because we could not accept the most basic gift of humanity: anxiety.

Many experts say that the most basic of human emotions is fear. I am not sure. Fear may be basic, but beneath fear lies anxiety. Fear has a symbol, an object, a vision. Anxiety lives with imagination and stems from mystery. Anxiety knows no object but must live with the many scenarios that drive the human will towards security.

Because society often dictates that fear is to be overcome or avoided, anxiety becomes captain of the vessel and drives us into the thick fog of night. Yet fear is neither good nor bad; it's simply part and parcel of the human condition. Accepting fear is respecting that which is greater than human achievement. Accepting fear is reverencing a power greater than what we have come to know.

We come into this world with three basic fears: the fear of abandonment, the fear of falling and the fear of loud noises.

The fear of abandonment
If you watch an infant, even though she doesn't have

consciousness or a great deal of mental development, you can sense the beginnings of the fear that Mom is not going to return. There is an emotion that precedes intellect. We are accustomed to being attached, and we no longer are. As we go further into our development, we experience what I call "the brokenness of life." In other words, we discover that at times, Mom is not there when we need her. Or help is not there when we need it. As a result, we develop a sense that maybe we're not going to be fed or held or cleansed.

As we grow through childhood, adolescence and adulthood, this fear doesn't change. Adults, the elderly, people who are financially secure, everyone lives with this fear. It's an ever-present danger. It becomes appropriately channeled or better managed, but it never goes away. There are no compensatory structures that help to somehow satiate our basic need to be connected. That's not to thwart our life choices or our excitement with life. But we live with it, and many of our reactions and behavioral choices are a byproduct or a response to the fear of abandonment.

Problems arise when we deny, overlook or diminish the power of this fear. As a counselor, I often hear, especially from men, "I don't fear abandonment." I disagree. We all fear abandonment. The key is understanding this fear, then finding some sort of internal power which allows us to find as much security as possible in the face of it.

I actually believe that the fear of abandonment is healthy precisely because it drives us to be connected. It keeps us needing, and it keeps us interdependent. Notice I didn't say dependent. I said interdependent, meaning united or attached. The function which this fear plays, then, is to keep us loving those people to whom we are connected, to love the structures that feed us and to be more dependent on connections than on independence. That's a good thing. Of course, our drive for connectedness can sometimes lead to hurt or disappointment. People will always fail us, make no mistake about it. But if we are willing to take the risk to be connected, to be interdependent, we will prevail far more times than we fail.

Think of the implications of this mindset in the business world or within your family. We now have an underlying system in place which says that it doesn't matter that you hurt me. I'm going to forgive, you're going to forgive and we're going to move on. That's because my fear of abandonment is not going to take over my desire to love, be connected and be attached. This mindset can also serve as a motivator to lead us to new ways of relating to one another. I don't think the business world does enough of this. We need to question each other, certainly, but we must exercise the greatest power we have, which is to trust each other. Trust is the only way we can begin to manage the fear of abandonment. If I trust you, I know that you will be there for me, that we're connected. When there is an abiding trust, the fear of abandonment is better managed.

The fear of falling

We are born with an instinctive fear that we are going to fall. Hence, we are driven to make sure the necessary support structures are in place. As we grow older, this fear doesn't change drastically. It changes subtly and transforms itself into the fear of failure. I think this also applies in terms of a nervous breakdown. This is actually a "falling" of the nervous system. We also talk about "going down the tubes" or "feeling down." There is something about being down that is frightening to humans. We don't want to be down. To be down is to experience a loss.

The fear of failure is also a fear of somehow losing my sense of security and ability to maintain myself. How am I going to be perceived, or how am I going to perceive myself, if I don't succeed in this particular project? Failure will throw my balance and my self-security off. The fear of failure is very personal. It's about me. It's about what am I in this world. It's about my struggle to find the balance which helps me stay propped up and to avoid a fall.

Balance is not running three miles and eating four salads every day. That's compulsive behavior. Balanced behavior is understanding the human condition, understanding that we are not perfect, not robots, not mechanical. We can't live so compulsively as to have everything set in stone. Life has to be lived in such a way that I step outside every once in a while and ask, "How am I doing in the face of this world, which is just as much in control of me as I am?" That becomes the question.

Jean Paul Sartre said, "Freedom is about doing with what you've been given." I believe that means we are only free to the degree that we understand our gifts and our shortcomings. I'm not free to be a center on a basketball team. Does that make me a failure? No. I make this judgment based on what I've been given.

Joe Smith is very good at creating. He's a visionary, and he can make things happen. But he's not a strong leader. He can't set boundaries. He understands these limitations, and he is determined not to allow his fear of failure to control his opportunities. Joe understands that past failures don't doom you to future failures. We grow into a sense of success. We can feel successful when we are at peace, when we are doing what's good for us and our world. Too often we tie success to money, college degrees and power, but in reality, success has nothing to do with any of those things. Do you know why? It is because the money, the things and the power are going to leave us. The key is figuring out what will make us happy. Can I find a balance in my life? Can I change the things that need to be changed in order to feel successful?

The fear of failure is a powerful motivator. It can also be a destructive force. This fear must be managed on every front. A leader, whether a parent or a teacher or a high school student who heads up his youth group at church, must learn that one's mission and point of reference for life cannot be whether he succeeded in the eyes of the economy or the power structures. It must be a question of succeeding vis a vis my goal. What did I want to do? And did I do it?

The fear of loud noises
Too many people dismiss this fear. In reality, it is actually the most pervasive of all fears because it is constant. The telephone rings at 2 a.m., and we learn that someone in the family is sick or has died. The phone rings at midnight to tell us our teenager has been in a car accident. The 9/11 terrorist attack on our nation. The fear of loud noises is actually a fear of anything that hits us from behind or takes us by surprise.

How do we manage loud noises? I don't know that we can. We have no power over what could happen each day. We wake up in the morning with Plan A, and by 10 a.m., we're at Plan D. If we're smart, we expected that to happen. I guess the only way one manages loud noises is to know they are going to come. The only control we have is our reaction to them.

I firmly believe that there are some benefits in loud noises, one of them being that they do throw us off. They do shake our serenity and our control. There's nothing wrong with being out of control sometimes. Being out of control can be a wonderful thing because at these moments, you really have to trust something higher. When that occurs, great things can happen. Throughout our early childhood and adolescence, we were rarely, if at all, informed that these fears, far from subsiding as we matured, would travel as constant companions, forever serving as reminders of life's yearly birthday gift of mortality.

Unformed in the faith of Uncertainty, we sought ways to buffer ourselves, creating the illusion that to be protected from harm's way, we must harm ourselves first. So we adopted a Defender of the Self, an inner critic, a saboteur, a self-destructive force that would be less painful than the pain inflicted by the outside world. Our Defender would be the optimal judge and jury, unceasing in its verdict of guilty. We learned that guilt would be our greatest defender from legitimate suffering. Guilt became our best friend, our favorite food, our prized possession. That is until the second paradox emerges: the voice of perfection.

The voice of perfection we developed as a result of external shame keeps us from experiencing the voice of Abiding Love. We resist Abiding Love, not with a will to do harm to life, but with an urgency to protect it. We choose the path of the critic, the saboteur, the self-destructive force. We slowly and systematically poison ourselves as a way of defending ourselves from life's suffering. Such a regimen does not necessarily lighten the burdens, but it does provide temporary relief. It provides the illusion of control.

At an early age, we begin to believe that we are deficient and deserving of harm, to the point that whenever attention is drawn to our true self, we cringe in fear of being exposed and shamed. The inner critic emerges, and all hell breaks loose within. To avoid the inner conflict, we find ways to become distracted. We use work and productivity, drama and vicarious living, addictions and compulsions. These diversions all seek to protect and defend the true self. No one ever begins to drink alcohol as a way to self-destruct. One drinks in order to ward off the loneliness of human encounters and perhaps to avoid abandonment.

No one ever chooses productivity as the road to the grave. One overworks because it provides a sense of security from a world filled with pitfalls and unseen dangers. It avoids the unforeseen loud noise.

No one ever chooses sexual exploits as a methodical form of suicide. One engages in exploits as a pathway to personal empowerment and self-esteem. To avoid falling.

To rediscover one's dignity and true light, one must move from the stage of early development of these defenses and advance to the level of true adulthood by surrendering to a God one has yet to meet. It is to say the words of Jesus: "Into your hands do I commend my spirit." It is to turn inward and be with one's self, without sword or shield. It is to "be" with peace.

In this surrender, we begin to witness the resurrection of a new self; a new way of thinking; a new way of speaking. This is a spiritual rite of adult passage missing in American society. In order to reach the stage of adulthood, one must stop doing and learn to be – all over again. It is the highest form of chivalry and the most optimal form of self-denial:
- To be with the inner critic within and allow God to name it.

- To be with the saboteur within and allow God to claim it.
- To be with the self-destructive force within and allow God to tame it.

This form of being is contrary to every rite of passage in today's society. We hardly hear words of preparation for "being" or a life of serenity. How often in the recent history of motivational speakers do we hear a plea to stop the search, to release oneself from the quest? How many people could even imagine adulthood as the stage of life when one actually slows down the drive to achieve? To become more? Who guides us to empty out instead of take in? Yet the tri-fold process that emerges from simply "being with oneself" can be a great pathway to lasting illumination and is, indeed, the hallmark of all great journeys taken by heroes. It is the passage that led them into a dark cave in order to eventually be brought into the light.

The inner protector is not the enemy of maturity and adulthood. But it can and will abort the process towards fullness of adult faith without the strength and guidance of the Voice of Abiding Love within. A voice that exerts itself when the "best," the "simplest," the most "natural" has been encouraged to be the first to speak. This Voice of Abiding Love forges an inner peace and acceptance of one's life as it is, not as one would have it. Not merely is this a conversion of a sword into the plowshare, for plowing for peace is not the essence of Abiding Love. Being with peace comes first.

"On the seventh day, He rested" indeed means that it is our "first" day, the Sabbath. On the first day, we rest. First things first, the voice of Abiding Love proclaims. Many of us have been formed with values that equate morning rising with busy-ness, beginning the day with planning, putting on the armor as we prepare to do battle with the world.

The voice of Abiding Love asks us to begin with inner peace, plan with inner peace, prepare with inner peace.
- Such a voice, once spoken and heard, can never be silent again.
- Such a voice, once accepted and internalized, converges with the Christ of salvation history.
- Such a voice no longer casts aspersions and judgments on the self or others but channels the inner forces toward a greater good: the betterment of the world. The false powers of busy-ness, drama and addiction give way to a serenity that takes one out of the self into a mission that, far from consuming the self, enlarges the scope of one's existence.

Such is the Voice of Abiding Love, a voice that asks us to look at our magnificence, our unending hope for a better world, our undaunted resilience during a crisis, our constant courage in the face of the uncontrollable, our willingness to meet a broken world daily, our compassion and outreach toward the weakest and most frail among us.

The Voice of Abiding Love appreciates both dissonance and harmony and allows the inner orchestra a chance to tune to its sound before attempting the next selection. In so doing, the Voice of Abiding Love validates integrity, motivates honesty and medicates hostility. The Voice of Abiding Love, far from overcoming the great fears, gives us the courage to put our engines in neutral and allow God to carry us through them into new life.

Such is peace. Such is serenity. Such is the Kingdom of God.

Water Your Own Grass

"The challenge is not to look outward and always wish for spring. No, it is to accept the need to care for our inner yards as they are..."

A friend recently dropped this glorious athem in the midst of a conversation: "If you think the grass is always greener on the other side, maybe you need to water your own." (Author unknown)

I could hear the melody for the rest of the day. So much so that I had to stop and reflect on the wisdom of the wordsmith who coined the simple yet profound philosophy of life. Not only was I struck by the turning of the camera inward to one's own yard, I was even more struck by the challenge to slow down the pace of the comparisons and put-downs we make on a habitual basis.

Everyone has a yard to maintain. The degree to which we care for our own inner yard radiates even through the harsh winter months when we think yards aren't worth caring for at all. I struggle with this as I look out my windows and want to close the curtains. I'd rather not be bothered with the yard until late March, or at least St. Patrick's Day. "Just let it be ugly," I say. "It's winter." And there is truth to that.

But the quote above challenges me to care for the yard, even in the ugly times of year. Perhaps even more so. Yards don't need a great deal of attention during this season, but they do need care. And while plants need less watering, they do, in fact, still need it.

Is the soul, mind, spirit and body not calling out for the same attention? We are forever pulled into the waxing and waning of fame and the glory of those lives we wish to emulate, even mimic. Our eyes turn green with envy at the sights and sounds of those who seem to have arrived or who are the glamor of the party scene, the belle of the ball or the Count of Monte Money. Trust me. My profession, in which I take great pride, tells me a different story and allows me to go behind the scenes of greener grass to expose their own winter doldrums. Everyone has their own crosses to bear.

The challenge is not to look outward and always wish for spring. No, it is to accept the need to care for our inner yards as they are, to water them, nurture them, tend to them during the flu season and find a way to focus our attention on who and where we are in life's great adventure.

Why Forgiveness Matters

"With honest reflection, we face the fact that everyone, regardless of their background or class, is an imperfect yet worthwhile human being who deserves to be favored with a forgiving attitude."

Time has honored no mystery greater than that of forgiveness. Theologians and philosophers have grappled with its complexity and power for centuries. Yet, even in today's world, few answers satisfy the human longing to resolve its ambivalent hold on us.

We value forgiveness, yet in the same breath, we wear grudges like a pair of old-but-loved shoes. Forgiveness, however we may amplify its importance, is distasteful to the palate of pleasure. We would rather chew on bitterness, smell silent revenge and drink the poison of resentment. Getting back at is often a greater force than moving forward, especially when we have entered the dark dungeon of feeling betrayed.

When we experience life's betrayals at an early age, we learn the art of striking back. Rain spoils our parade, wind knocks us off our bike, bullies kick us from behind and friends gossip about us. Those who love us inadvertently throw us under the bus, and we learn that we must defend ourselves from hurt and pain. We also internalize, rightly or wrongly, that we somehow are to blame for the pain around us.

Many children, exposed to the dangers of the world, take on a responsibility and an expectation that "only if I ..." The young and primitive brain kicks in: We wish to find a way to survive, to feel a shield of protection and power. We don't know how to release our anger and fear, and when we look for models of coping, we see little if any genuine forgiveness. Hearing the tone with which the often-spoken phrase, "I forgive but I won't forget," is communicated, we know that the statement spells cynicism more than truth. We quickly internalize the need to wear the armor of self-protection in our quest for safety.

Whether it be roaming through the house of loathing, renting the apartment of silent treatment or employing words that harm another's self-image, life becomes about self-protection. Forgiveness of a perceived wrongdoing, however inaccurate the perception may be, is parked in a lot far away. If and when we are graced to gradually peel away the layers of our fears and protective instincts learned as a child, we begin to realize another truth: that no one is immune from hurt, from suffering, from life's afflictions. With honest reflection, we face the fact that everyone, regardless of their background or class, is an imperfect yet worthwhile human being who deserves to be favored with a forgiving attitude. The due diligence eventually leads us to self-evaluation, and we become aware that the most important person to forgive is our very self.

Just as life inflicts harm on us, we accept the hurt inflicted upon others. We've lied, cheated, stolen, judged, scorned and violated other people's rights. Our rational abilities lead us to the conclusion that if we can't forgive ourselves, how can we forgive others? So why does forgiveness matter? Put simply, if we can't find motivations other than anger, revenge or cynicism from which to live, we'll never reach forgiveness. There will be good reason to conclude that we will have become little more than walking zombies.

When life hurts us or we hurt another life, we have the choice of two paths. We can take steps to move beyond the hurt and reinvest in life, or we can become frozen in bitterness, self-loathing and self-pity. It is, indeed, a matter of life and death.

Hell has been cast as raging, eternal flames. But perhaps ice is a better image. To become so frozen that the heart barely pumps is to tragically commit a slow but steady suicide, either into drugs, work, sex, greed, relational drama, violence or emotional isolation. Life is a roller coaster of interactions and relationships. To be a member of society, we must accept that the very interactions that are at the heart of joyful living are also the very core of hurt and pain. To experience genuine forgiveness, we cease looking for an end to scars because they are permanent or playing the game of persecutor and victim who are both doomed to fail. We must surrender our power to forgive over to a higher power and continue to believe in life, love and service.

In surrendering, we become resolved in meditation that the pain we are currently experiencing must be held and healed, that life can find rebirth from suffering and death and that whatever revenge there is can be transformed into a desire for growth, acceptance and new behaviors that will lead to a deeper peace and joy. So we pray for the one who hurts us and ask a power greater than self to guide him or her on their own path of growth and forgiveness of self.

With such a change of attitude, the question becomes not so much why forgiveness matters, but how life could matter at all without it. Why does forgiveness matter? Because ultimately, it slows down the wrinkling of the soul and cleans out the arteries of the spirit.

Hallmarks of the Real Self

"Life is not a series of random choices and relativity. The self is more analogous to an apple with a core than an onion whose layers lead to emptiness."

After attending a seminar on Post Traumatic Stress Disorder and learning a great deal about perceived versus real threats, I began to question other avenues where what is "perceived" and what is "real" could be clearly delineated. I realized that while perception may be reality, there is much about our perceptions that needs to be put on trial, questioned as hostile witnesses, put to the test of logic. In other words, perception is not always reality; very often, it comes from a history that needs to be placed in a box and if not trashed, at least placed in the attic for posterity.

Perceived threat comes from past pain and therefore has us asking questions such as, "What if this happens?" "Could it lead to that?" "What could come of it?" "Where will it lead?" Valid questions, perhaps, but all steeped in a sense of concern that the future will not bode well.

At the age of 18, when still an adolescent myself, I took a course in adolescent psychology. Vividly I recall following the professor after class one day and asking him, "What is the real self, and how does one know what is real and authentic about one's self? Is there a real self, or is it all a matter of perception? Are choices made from a 'core,' or are they all relative to the context?"

The questions, although offered in various ways, seemed pretty straightforward to me, and even though they seem somewhat ethereal as I look back, I remember waiting for an answer like a puppy waiting for a treat. This highly respected professor was about to provide me with an answer to life's puzzle. But he didn't. Rather, he looked at me and said that I needed to continue searching within and that the true self is unique to each person. It was uniquely developed, uniquely evolving and uniquely transformative. One's real self couldn't be defined or delineated by anyone or anything outside one's own journey inward. He said that in time, I would become comfortable with the core of my being.

Having reflected for the past 40 years on both his answer and my own life experiences, I have come to believe that the professor was partially correct. While life is a unique journey into one's authenticity and self-consciousness, there are some hallmarks that will guide us into self-discovery and therefore into healthy living.

Life is not a series of random choices and relativity. The self is more analogous to an apple with a core than an onion whose layers lead to emptiness. I offer a few of these hallmarks in an attempt to assist in the development of a real as opposed to a perceived self.

- The real self experiences a wide range of emotions that are often blended and integrated. There is no way to reduce one's experience to a singular emotion at a time. Very often, our feelings are like a fine meal. There are several flavors blended into one. We can feel sad and mad at the same time. We can feel joy, excitement, fear and courage all in one. This is the real self.

- The real self is entitled. It is entitled to human dignity, respect, compassion, attention, validation, mastery over tasks and simple pleasures.

- The real self is motivated from within and active in identifying needs, wishes, dreams, goals and frustrations. Most importantly, the real self is driven not by outside forces, but by a strong value system that resists the temptation to seek approval, status or power over another.

- The real self is able to adapt, cope with problems in a positive manner and soothe one's body without the need for constant self-medication.

- The real self resists the temptation to wallow in misery, blame the world for problems and re-enact old experiences in an effort to change them. Rather, the real self is intentional and grounded in the moment. It flows with life, believes in its resilience, feels secure and safe in the world and makes every effort to navigate through the storms of life knowing that this, too, shall pass.

- The real self is consistent in word and deed. The words match the behaviors. The values voiced match the choices made. The depth of character guides the decision-making process and is resolved once a decision is made.

- The real self is alert, but not hyper-alert, vigilant but not hyper-vigilant, cautious at times but not overly careful, firm but not set in stone, clear but not obstinate, goal-oriented but not abusive to another's rights.

- The real self is defined by a deep and abiding set of morals that are the compass from which all directions are mapped out. The real self is able to discern between which societal values are steeped in human dignity and which are steeped in primitive fear and has no problem being counter-cultural when society's inclinations are either outdated or simply wrong.

These are but a few of what constitutes the real self for me, and if I were to run into the professor from my college days, I would tell him how grateful I was that he empowered me to make the journey within as a means to finding myself. I make no pretense to fully living out these core concepts each day, but I do continue in an imperfect way to strive for their fruition and hope you will at least give them consideration in your journey toward serenity and peace.

Slow Down

"When did having a strong work ethic mean that we are never off the clock? Always available? Responding to the next interruption demanding immediate attention lest we decrease in the next approval ratings?"

Does anyone remember the great Simon and Garfunkel tune from 1966? "Slow down, you move too fast," they implored.

Too many people come into my office in high gear. Now admittedly, I often find myself pushing the pedal and, without looking at my gas tank, find myself running on near-empty. Why, I ask. Why is our pace so incredibly fast? Why are we so stubbornly insistent on adding more to the plate? Getting more accomplished in a day? Wishing for more hours?

I don't know the ultimate answer, but I have a strong suspicion that underneath all of the pedal-pushing, sixth-gear, over-the-speed-limit movement is the belief that it's never enough. I'm never enough. I don't have enough. The grades are not good enough. My salary is not good enough. The projects are not done well enough. There isn't enough satisfaction.

Simply "feeling groovy" is just too '60s and way too slow for the world of today.

We may say that life today is much more complicated and stressful than in any other period in history. It's easy to rebuke my philosophical underpinnings by saying that I don't understand the stresses and demands placed on today's life. Many will argue that without driving and pushing the pedal, we're unable to provide for our families, fulfill our needs and satisfy our way of life. Some will even argue that without the drive, we become complacent, lazy, **boring and stale. Really?**

When did having a strong work ethic mean that we are never off the clock? Always available? Responding to the next interruption demanding immediate attention lest we decrease in the next approval ratings?

To all of the above arguments, I ask these basic questions:
- When is enough, enough?
- When does what we need become what we want?
- When does our appetite for more weigh us down, both literally and figuratively?
- When are we off the clock, resting and relaxing, wearing the silk robe of being rather than the iron mask of doing?

We are the most overweight people on earth, have the largest number of storage centers in the universe, can't make closets large enough to hold the clothes from which we haven't removed tags and believe the more pills we take, the better we'll feel.

It's just never enough, until a crisis comes along, and we hopefully face the dark reality that we've been chasing an illusion and start a pathway to recovery. Too often we speak of addiction as drugs, sex, work, food. But these are merely the pathways taken. The true addiction at the core of all abuse is wanting what we want when we want it. This ultimately means, I am not enough with what I am or what I have.

Alcoholics Anonymous asks us to "keep it simple." The Buddha asks us to "be detached." Jesus says if we have two coats, share one with a poor person. With each day that comes to an end I tell myself that I am pleased enough. That I am good enough. That I love enough. That I worked hard enough. That I accomplished enough. And I put my life in neutral, asking God to give me rest so that I can rise tomorrow and once again, in my limited way, attempt to make a difference in the lives of those I meet.

In the morning that comes, I ask God to pace my day so that I don't miss out on the truly important and meaningful opportunities that I pass along the way. I ask God to give me a vision that moves, not at the speed of sound or light, but at the speed of humanity. For I much prefer being human. Too much sound becomes noise which blocks my hearing. Too much light becomes overbearing and blinds me to simple pleasures.

Several years ago, I was presenting a parenting workshop. A woman walked up to me at the break and told me a story I have never forgotten.

She said that she had two boys, one in 9th grade and one in 7th. The week prior to the workshop was spring break for the boys, and they asked for the plan for the time off. Their mother told them that she would take them for dinner at a nice restaurant and that they could order whatever they wanted.

When the evening arrived and they were seated at the restaurant, one of the sons complained that his friend was at Disneyworld. The other chimed in with his dissatisfaction, voicing that his best friend was on the beach. They weren't happy about the state of their lives' affairs. Their mother smiled and mildly responded, "Yes, and we have this wonderful restaurant," to which they both fumed and retorted that it was a pathetic alternative and nothing to be excited about.

With that, she said what I have come to believe was one of the most powerful statements ever: "Yes, and if you can't enjoy this experience, what makes you think you would enjoy the beach? Or Disneyworld? If you can't be grateful for what you have now, what makes you think you will ever be grateful?"

What a great mom; what a great philosophy. What a great way of saying, "Let this be enough."

Slow down, gang. We're moving too fast.

Vulnerability, Authenticity and Humility: A Trinitarian Formula

"There would be no trying out for the role. There would be only the decision to audition for it or not. There would be no great disappointment if not chosen. There would be satisfaction in running the race."

Some years ago, a therapist asked me to try to pick up a pen. I picked it up. He said, "No, I said to try to pick it up." I picked it up again. And again, with greater force, he urged me to try to pick it up. By then, I got the message. I either picked up the pen or I didn't. There was no trying.

A few short weeks ago, I considered trying out for the lead role in the upcoming *Les Miserables* production in our local community theater. It had been nearly 40 years since I played a role in a stage show, but being a closet actor wannabe, the voices continued to pound in my head: "Give it a shot. What have you got to lose?" Remembering the words of the very influential therapist, I realized that there would be no trying out. I would audition for the role or not. Simple as that. And why now? Why this show? Why at this age? Because without a doubt, there is more sage within me than saboteur, more confidence in my abilities than ever before and more humility as to my limits and my status in the face of far greater voices than my own.

The year was 1986, summer time, and I was discerning my next chapter in life. What better way to discern than to take a trip to Europe with monies saved up over the past five years?

A 12-day tour of some of the great cities ended with a few days in London. Waking up on the first day, I was out and about early, walking the streets on another day of discovery, when I noticed a very long line wrapped around a busy corner. With great anticipation, I made my way to the marquis above the doorway. The visual was unforgettable, both near and far. It read *Les Miserables.* Without thinking, I began my quest for tickets to see a show I had heard nothing about and knew not what it involved. I just knew I had to see it that night.

With a lot of work and even more luck, I found two tickets in the nosebleed section. But I didn't care. With binoculars, I would experience something that countless people were talking about.

And so it was the experience of a lifetime. I cried to the sound of Fontaine's "I Dreamed a Dream" and watched her die. I trembled hearing Colm Wilkinson pray "Bring Him Home." To this day, there has never been an experience quite like that. I had been converted by the power of the statement, "To love another is to see the face of God." So now you know the rest of the story, or at least of that chapter.

Come with me to the present time, more than 25 years later, and imagine my desire to enter into the footsteps of Jean Valjean here at home. But I am a different man than in 1986. There would be no trying out for the role. There would be only the decision to audition for it or not. There would be no great disappointment if not chosen. There would be satisfaction in running the race. There would be no sizing up of the competition, only doing my best at the time and leaving the results in the hands of capable judges.

I decided to audition for the role. With no arrogance, I made it clear that such was all I was interested in. If I wasn't the man for the role, so be it.

The audition went well, and I sang "For Once in my Life" with a deep conviction and passion. I was offered a chance to return the next night at 6 p.m., given music and told to be prepared to sing those selected pieces.

The next day was busy, and I found the stress of the music and the investment of time and energy was already causing me to second guess my decision. You know the saying, "Be careful what you ask for. You just might get it."

I was there at 6 p.m. along with well over 100 others wanting a spot in the show. The director informed us before beginning the auditions that 16 men and 13 women would be selected. I looked around the room and became acutely aware of what actors go through in New York: audition after audition with far more no's than nods.

But suddenly, I was relaxed and at peace. In fact, I was moved by all the details of the moment. With all of its faults, our nation prizes not only competition but the freedom to gather peaceably. All of these people, young and old, male and female, rich and poor, were competing, not for money or beauty, but for the chance to sing and act, for a chance to be a part of perhaps the most celebrated pop opera in American history.

Then the tide turned. We were told that those auditioning for Jean Valjean should sit back and relax, read a book or play a game on the iPhone. We would be the last to be heard. And the wait began.

For nearly four hours, I waited, listening to some marvelous voices in the adjoining room, chatting with a few of the contestants and wondering who in that room was my competition.

The hour finally came, and nearly a dozen of us were called into the audition room to make our case and plead our cause through song and stage presence.

My audition went poorly, and after hearing voice after voice, my hopes faded and aspirations dimmed. There were many much more suitable men vying for the role. A few were asked to stay, and the rest of us walked out mostly in silence. Some might conclude that we were all sad and forlorn, disappointed and carrying crushed egos. But I didn't get that feeling.

Yes, we were all a bit disappointed, no doubt. But I also felt an incredible sense of pride in all of us for taking the leap, for rolling the dice, for believing in ourselves and in our craft and for trusting that the directors would choose the most suitable for such an ambitious task.

T.S. Elliott once said that "we had the experience but missed the meaning." Not so for me that wonderful night. I was proud to know that there are so many talented people right here in our neighborhood; I was honored to be among a dozen incredible voices whose very presence challenged me to do my best; I was amazed at the passion and patience with which people sat through a lengthy process; and most of all, I was reignited by the power of the theater to change lives and make a difference in the ways of this world.

Most of us have either heard the music or seen the show. We know the storyline of how a man was sent to prison for stealing a loaf of bread and how he was converted by a loving bishop. We know that on that night, he made a pact with God to fight for justice and lead with compassion.

When it came time for me to audition, I was tired and less

certain of myself in the role and the time it would consume but not hesitant with regard to the power of the lyrics and melody. With conviction, I sang what has been over the years a defining pen in the crafting of my story. Arriving at home that night, I was neither sad nor jealous. Rather I was at peace. Finally, I had come to full terms with one of the great statements of faith: "Do the best you can, make the best choice you can, and then leave the results to God."

There are no greater rewards that can come to those who follow this tenet, for it is the tenet of authenticity, humility and vulnerability: a Trinitarian formula made in Heaven.

Choose to Refuse to Excuse

"As we develop, we also begin to tolerate certain levels of stress and anxiety. We begin living more in the moment, in a state of mindfulness of the Now, knowing that feelings will pass, predictability will grow and resilience will befriend us."

Let's face it: Many if not most of us struggle with self-regulation. Yet, this is a key ingredient to not simply controlling aggression but, more importantly, to living with peace of mind and peace of heart. Let's break it down in simple terms.

We have what is known as stress-response systems, or monitors that sense and send alarms to the brain when something is going wrong. Naturally, we then seek ways to get what we need to lower the sounding alarm.

As children, we are generally unaware, but during the developmental years, we are educated about the ways in which we can regulate our responses. These are what I call the skills of life management. When mentors (parents, teachers, coaches) are empowering, we are encouraged to take an active role in our emotional formation, just as we would with learning the building blocks of mathematics or science. With "good enough" teachers and environments, we actively learn to self-regulate and to release our emotions appropriately. And that's the key: appropriately.

Given that we are all in different developmental phases, genetically as well as environmentally unique, life becomes a constant game. We roll the dice with our responses, searching out ways that will protect us as well as well as care for those with whom we share this globe. Therefore, what is appropriate will forever be a judgment call that leaves us in existential angst: We are alone in our decisions, but with proper nurturing and confidence building, can learn to live with them as "good enough."

Even so, our stress-response systems can become better organized over time and less hyper-reactive, particularly in the adult years. We can re-parent ourselves. Whether we had or didn't have "good enough" environments to help us develop skills for managing frustration and tolerating our inability to get what we want or need, we are not old dogs learning new tricks. We are human beings capable of both unlearning old behaviors and learning new ones. Yes, at any age, we can learn to self-regulate.

At some point in our lives, starting as early as we possibly can, we can choose to refuse to excuse our actions through genetic predisposition, developmental problems or parental environment. Regardless of the apparent results of these poor environmental factors – lack of impulse control, hypersensitivity to transitions and a tendency to overreact to minor challenges or stressors – we can change.

What we need most in developing self-regulation is specific praise, new daily structures, sleep hygiene (early to bed and early to rise makes a man healthy, wealthy and wise), proper nutrition, exercise, healthy environments in which to experiment with new behaviors, enrichment through the arts and a healthy community to help us manage the chaotic feelings that will arise as a result of creating a new normal. In doing so, we are able to resolve past wounds that have hindered our self-confidence and write a new chapter in our book of life.

The more developed we become, the more we are able to deal with the challenges of life. We can learn to adapt to rainy days, to find options when life throws up roadblocks, to measure our reaction against the situation and to weigh and discern the value of the response against the consequence. In a very paradoxical way, we give up our control in order to learn how to control in a more healthy way.

As we develop, we also begin to tolerate certain levels of stress and anxiety. We begin living more in the moment, in a state of mindfulness of the Now, knowing that feelings will pass, predictability will grow and resilience will befriend us. We learn that freedom is no longer doing what I think I should do out of compliance to old fears and trauma; rather, freedom is about what I do with what I am given in the here and now, and that while I can't control my environment, I am no longer a child who is dependent upon the grownups. I am a grown up.

With each challenge, we seek to make the next right choice, and the alarm that once went off to protect now signals us to reward. With self-reward comes a new pattern and a new pathway to expertise. What was once threatening is now seen as an opportunity to become a master of self-regulation.

Here are a few tips for becoming a master of self-regulation:

    1. Accentuate the positive first, and be sincere.
    2. Use humor and wit to get through difficult moments.
    3. Ask a simple question before behaving: Am I reacting, or am I responding?
    4. Deflate the ego by telling yourself that another's behavior is about them, not you.
    5. Always have a plan and stick with it, even if you

have to change it from time to time to accommodate the unexpected.

6. Take care of yourself by saying no to your wants and the need for immediate gratification. Say no to others without feeling guilty.
7. Count the times you say yes to other's requests, and reward yourself for your kindness.
8. Reflect backwards and plan forward.
9. Have courage to confront an issue without confronting the dignity of the person.
10. No name calling (either to self or others).
11. Change the environment if you feel you are being triggered to an unhealthy behavior or old response.
12. Rest, relax, unwind and rewind. No one should be on alert 24-7.
13. Create a habit of looking for options.
14. Walk away and calm down.
15. Ask yourself, "What's so urgent? Can it wait?"
16. Have a support group that gives objective feedback.
17. Practice passive listening: "Your ears will never get you in trouble." (Frank Tygen)
18. Practice active listening: This is being engaged with the speaker and mirroring back what is heard and often what has not been said. I have a quote in my office that reads, "Listening to what is often unsaid." But offering no advice.
19. Slow down. If there was ever a need for slowing down, it's in today's American society. Tell yourself that it's not that urgent. Will it really matter in a few years? Is it worth the strain on the heart? What's the rush? If you answer honestly, you will start laughing at yourself and will be back to being human again.
20. Learn assertiveness skills. Become responsible for your actions but not the results. Become aware of the

difference between consequences of one's actions and the results of making conscious, reasonable and healthy choices. In other words, make the best choice you can, and then give it over to God.

21. Develop emotional boundaries: Someone getting angry doesn't mean you have to get angry back.

22. Pray the serenity prayer often: "Lord, grant me the serenity to accept the things I cannot change, the courage to change the things I can and the wisdom to know the difference."

23. Avoid people who bring out your worst, without judging them.

24. Learn to endure suffering and hurt by practicing unpleasant duties.

25. Practice stewardship: We pass through but once, and we don't take it with us. My favorite line is from a preacher: "I ain't never seen a U-Haul on the back of a hearse."

26. Practice acceptance of things as they are and not as you would have them.

27. Be direct and not sideways. Don't dump on your children the anger you are experiencing toward your wife or your boss.

28. Discern between which bridges to close and which ones to repair.

29. Remember, you are the only one in your life you are with 24/7. Learn to love and accept yourself, especially your shortcomings.

30. Always have something to look forward to.

From Betrayal to Forgiveness: A Love Story

"What makes betrayal so evil is that it can be committed only by those in whom we put our trust and faith. Betrayal can't breathe unless its oxygen comes from a place of perceived safety. We're never betrayed by our enemies."

Forgiveness is a word that is often tossed around. We hear it in churches and synagogues. Whether someone portends to be a devout Christian or an avowed atheist, the desire to forgive is omnipresent. The problem is that we would rather toss it than catch it.

We hear phrases like "forgive and forget," "forgive but never forget," "to err is human; to forgive, divine." Alcoholics Anonymous asks us to promptly admit when a wrong has been committed and even more promptly ask for forgiveness. Even though we're not quite sure how to reach this seemingly far-off planet of forgiveness, with eternal hope, we desire this road that we're told leads to peace. We want to believe that there is a promise that comes with forgiveness. Ironically, we know that without putting down the shield and letting forgiveness hold us, the anchor we cling to will cause us to drown in a cesspool of bitterness.

What we often don't know, or at least don't want to know, is that forgiveness is perhaps the singularly most critical pathway toward unconditional love that we will experience on this earth. Which is why we need to stop tossing it. But the package is filled with treacherous forces, and we can't begin to experience forgiveness until we've been battered by the brutal power of betrayal.

Some forms of forgiveness are inexpensive. They don't cost very much. Small hurts and mistakes which are neither unintentional nor mean spirited can be eased with little cost to one's self-preservation. But betrayal eats away the flesh of one's very dignity. Betrayal is a dagger in the back that cannot be taken out without further pain. A sword that cuts the person's worth in half, betrayal leaves a trail of blood.

Betrayal is a husband discovering that his wife has been cheating for years while masking it with the brilliance of an Academy Award winner; a trusting child left unprotected against the wilds of predators whose threats of retaliation, if spoken of, bear down like iron masks; walking into a home to find the note and the empty closet; investing in a company for years only to be replaced with not a word of thanks; riding the roller coaster of business partnership for decades to find that at the end, the cost of the ride wasn't evenly distributed. Betrayal is discovering that after years of providing relief, alcohol, opiates and pornography are out to secretly and slowly destroy us. Betrayal is giving the nod to another's best and receiving the worst as payback. It is the butterfly that, after winning our trust, shows us it is a wasp.

What makes betrayal so evil is that it can be committed only by those in whom we put our trust and faith. Betrayal can't breathe unless its oxygen comes from a place of perceived safety. We're never betrayed by our enemies. We can only be betrayed by those to whom we entrust ourselves.

Therein lies the human dilemma.

If those we trust can and will hurt us, how can we ever experience unconditional love? If betrayal is a foregone conclusion that will eventually knock on every door, what else is there but to build walls around our souls and live in a prison of loneliness? So we hide in closets with books, lie in the dark staring into space, crying endlessly from the pain, and swim in a cesspool of addictions and compulsions, only to discover that there is no real place of safety. Betrayal is in the very air we breathe.

In fact, the ultimate betrayal is toward the self. We begin to consider ourselves unworthy of life, liberty and happiness and choose to distrust not only the world, but our own judgments.

Show me someone who has not been betrayed in life, and I'll show you a frightened liar. No one is denied the experience of a broken trust. Show me someone who does not blame himself for the betrayal, and I'll show you a heart of stone. No one is immune from self-loathing. We've all had to walk the darkened path and live with one eye over our shoulder and the other eye set to maneuvering the next footstep in order to avoid the unseen explosive device. Some of us face it. Others deny it. Either way, we have a propensity to trust neither friend nor foe, neither self nor other, neither the present nor the future. Betrayal kills the soul and leaves one so bruised that the only pathway to self-preservation appears to be "trust no one, including yourself."

And so now we know why forgiveness is the only pathway to real love and the most difficult toward which to commit. Forgiveness is a divine vision that sees past the warts and through the selfish tendencies. Forgiveness knows that danger lurks but offers the grace to laugh in its face and continue to dance despite the mines all around us.

Forgiveness sees beauty and goodness beyond the pain and the spiritual resurrection that blasts through the prison of revenge and loves even more deeply. It is the alpha and the omega of adulthood: when we move beyond asking "why me" and start answering "thank you for life." Forgiveness is getting back on the saddle after a broken arm, back in the pool after nearly drowning, back in the game even though you know in the end, you will lose. It is reaching out and trusting all over again; going back to the stove after being burned. Paradoxically, it is walking down the path where we were most wounded but doing so without the illusion of false security.

Forgiveness is going neither backwards to repair the wrong nor sideways to unload on someone else. Rather, it is a giant leap into the unknown future.

It is neither a reconciling with nor a returning to in order fix the broken trust; rather, it is a flight out of the nest of safety with broken wings into the bliss of a new adventure, not caring that our flight has been humbled. Forgiveness is the gift of risk and vulnerability. It is the pathway to angelic living, offering us the weight of wounded angels in flight with no resentment weighing us down.

Without forgiveness, we become the walking dead, never trusting and forever vigilant. Without forgiveness, we live with an uncontrollable fear of the next hurt. In doing so, we put our stock in processes and substances that neither calm nor ease the wound. Embracing forgiveness, however, is embracing brokenness and accepting humanity as it is and not as we would have it.

Some will say we were created to move more closely to being divine; I say we were created to move more closely to being human. And the only way we can ever know true humanity is to move through betrayal toward forgiveness, not with the false power of arrogance or pride but with the strength of Samson and the wisdom of Solomon, the faith of Miriam and the courage of Joan of Arc.

We truly cannot speak of being loving people without also being forgiving people. We will never become the rose without accepting the bitter snows.

Christmas: A Season for Higher Standards

"I am ... suggesting that we think back to what really matters as a pilgrim people who pass this way but once, who have but one coin to spend and no limitless credit card."

Some say the musical standards of the '30s and '40s are deemed such because they outlast time itself. Those of us of a certainly age could hardly imagine a world without *Fly Me to the Moon* or *Misty*. Forever sung, forever adored, the standards are our popular classics.

Imagine Christmas without *A Christmas Song, White Christmas* or *Silent Night*. I look forward to singing these standards during the holidays: songs for all ages and all generations.

At a recent gig, 21-year-old young lady asked if I could sing *Pennies from Heaven*. After getting through the shock of her awareness of the tune, I pulled out the jewel and sang it with all of my heart. It was a great moment, a precious memory, a hopeful song that will never die.

But so much for music.

What about life's standards? Those tried-and-true values and habits that we engaged in back when time seemed to move more slowly and rituals were appreciated; when respectful standards were just that: standard for all towns, all cities and all states. Isn't Christmas a season to bring out and dust off those standards?

I'm speaking of the proper ways to act, the appropriate and respectful deeds that used to come naturally, the time-honored values and family rituals that too many of us have lost from our enslavement to consumerism.

I may be getting old and showing my age by reminiscing, but I recall a time when:

- We all had chores on Saturday.
- We spoke respectfully to elders and would never use profanity, either in private or public.
- We painted the bedroom together with our parents.
- We made our beds and helped when a sibling was sick.
- We stood when elders walked into the room.
- We greeted everyone we met, stranger or friend, with a smile and an attitude of caring.
- We washed our cars on Sunday afternoon and played touch football in the backyard until dark.
- We played without the latest gadgets and used our imagination.
- We dressed up on Sunday because, as my father would say, "It's Sunday."
- We respected Sunday as a day of rest and worship; if we needed something, we borrowed from a neighbor because the stores were closed.
- We visited the sick and buried the dead.
- We rode around the neighborhood during Advent looking at the decorations.
- We spent a day at Goldsmith's in Memphis, where my father sat on Santa's lap, and we laughed at his childlike qualities.
- We went through closets at Thanksgiving and gave clothing to St. Vincent de Paul as a Christmas gift to the poor.
- We accepted "hand me downs" and wore them with gratitude.
- We had dessert but once a week and only on Sunday, usually my mother's prized banana pudding.
- We were on the altar boys' schedule and once every

few months, had to rise at 5:30 a.m. to serve at daily mass.
- We said please, thank you, you're welcome and I'm sorry.
- We honored the liturgical seasons, prayed as a family several nights a week and always had Holy Water at the door in which we dipped our fingers and made the sign of the cross.
- We said the Our Father, Hail Mary and Glory Be each morning on the way to school.
- We revered our civic leaders, spiritual leaders and school teachers as the highest of all professions.
- We spent once a month in Church for a "Holy Hour" during the middle of the night where we would sit or kneel in silence and appreciate the mystery of the Transcendent.
- We put whatever change we had in a jar on the counter and when full, counted the coins. On a special night, we would then have shrimp and steak, precious commodities in a struggling household.
- We would hear our father ask the creditor, "Can I pay it monthly?" and hear the creditor say, "Of course." And he did, sometimes $5 a month until paid.
- We were taught the only thing that mattered in life was your good name, which meant, "Be honest, be fair to all and pay your bills."
- We would argue, fuss and fight but rise the next morning to greet a new dawn and begin anew as a family of redeemed sinners.
- We would work at the annual Parish Fair and raise enough money to subsidize our small Catholic school.
- We would have a "pantry night," when all the church-goers would bring canned goods from which the Sisters of Charity of Nazareth would find nourishment throughout the school year.

- As we got older, we each formed personal values steeped in a tradition of unconditional love and acceptance.
- We appreciated Church, not as a set of dogma or rules but as a community of sinners, one no better than the other, who used the scriptures not as a pole to lean upon but as a beam to enlighten our path and who believed that tradition was about sharing what we had, not judging the less fortunate.

I am not saying that we need to get back to pantry filling or even 2 a.m. Holy Hours. Nor am I recommending that everyone be Catholic or even Christian, for that matter.

I am, however, suggesting that we think back to what really matters as a pilgrim people who pass this way but once, who have but one coin to spend and no limitless credit card.

Could there be more to Sundays than we dare imagine? Is there not a place in our selfish lives for a Sabbath? A day of rest and relaxation, a day of being aware of something larger than our small and short-lived days on earth? Pick a day. Any day.

Could there be more owed to manners and polite society than we think? Could there be more to the simple values and pleasures that come from a simpler way of life? Could there be something said for ordinary time and extraordinary time? For when everything is special, is anything special? If every event is extraordinary, is anything extraordinary?

I come from a time when life was different, when our hands were our phones and the sun was our clock; a time when instead of being a consumer family, we were an economic system where we all owned a piece of the rock and showed it by being respectful and involved in its upkeep.

How I long for such a time. How I long for those timeless standards to return.

Perhaps this Christmas could be the time when Christmas standards are not only thought of as songs, but as habits that feed the eternal soul.

A Counter-Culture Christmas

"I treasure the feeling I had in awakening to the reality that all over the country, ... my family members were taking delight in a counter-cultural Christmas: a gift that had a higher price tag than anything else I value, that of time."

Many years ago, our family opened the door to the angel of death. My mother passed away as the result of a brain aneurysm. We buried her on January 3, 2001.

A few short years later, we sold our childhood home and moved our father into an assisted-living facility.

My mother had a knack for saving mementoes of the milestones of her eight children and eleven grandchildren. As we cleaned out the house and discarded the things of this world, the many pictures and news clippings of these events found their way to my storage closet. Stacked high were 20 albums in which she had saved 51 years' worth of the proudest moments of her family's life. A devoted mother and wife, the albums were testimony to what she honored; memories made of those in which she had invested her entire adult life.

I'm not sure what prompted me to pull the 20 albums out of the closet. Not known for completing overwhelming projects or for living with the resulting mess in my small dining/living area for six weeks, I can only attest to divine intervention. For pull them I did, two weeks prior to Thanksgiving.

With Christmas already on my mind, it was done. It was decided. It was resolved. I would make 20 piles of pictures and news clippings – one for each child, grandchild and, of course, my then 84-year-old father. This would be my

Christmas gift to the family. No spending of money, no purchasing of more things to clutter homes, no buying into consumerism. This Christmas was to be spent reminiscing, offering up time and emotion, being with my mother and creating a Christmas gift that came from both my heart and hers.

The project took nearly two hours out of each day for the following month, after which I then selected which memento would go to each person. It was no small task, as many pictures had more than one family member, and I had to carefully balance who would receive what, making the giving fair and impartial. Once that challenge was met, there was the question of presentation. But I realized there was no need to purchase new albums. Why not use the old, I thought, creating another symbol and allowing for another walk down memory lane? You see, my mother kept the albums in a prominent place in the den, allowing anyone who entered to browse through her family history.

After completing the project, I wrapped each album and mailed them with the request that they not be opened until the very end of the Christmas unwrapping ritual.

On Christmas morning, my Father and sister Angela, who were spending Christmas with me, opened their special gifts and, amidst tears, were overwhelmed by their life placed before them through the love of their wife and mother. I treasure the feeling I had in awakening to the reality that all over the country, from Houston to Memphis, my family members were taking delight in a counter-cultural Christmas: a gift that had a higher price tag than anything else I value, that of time.

The project cost me nearly 50 hours of time, more than

a work week. If I had the chance to do it all over again, I would welcome the opportunity. For few memories are greater than those moments when the calls came: "Thank you, Nicky, for an unbelievable gift, a lasting treasure."

I'm not sure if it made a major difference in their lives, but it certainly reminded me of one of the true meanings of Christmas, not experienced by spending money, but rather by spending time. I'm thinking that for the next Christmas gift to my loved ones, I will take them all on a cruise, asking them to avoid spending money on gifts and taking it with them to enjoy with the family.

Because of the price of taking 20 or more (some are marrying) family members on a cruise, it might be another five years before it occurs. And that's okay. I'd rather look forward to that than to simply spend on the moment.

Retailers will surely reject my reasoning behind last year's gift, as it does nothing to promote society's values. But then again, many say Christianity is supposed to be counter-cultural. Whether or not that is true, I know that such giving fulfilled, nourished and added to my understanding of Christmas.

Did I make an album for myself? No. Pictures and news clippings have all been stuffed in a box and returned to the same closet. My plan is to pull out the box on Black Friday. When everyone else is looking for bargains, I intend to spend the day with my mother and her memories of me growing up.

Angel of Death or Angel of Grace?

"These bells of human longing ring most shallow for those who are at death's door, who while yearning for something more are never really ready to leave what they have."

January and February are the dreary months of the year. There's little doubt that many of us will pass on during these months. Death seems so common during the dead of winter.

Just the other night, I had the gift of traveling with a priest to anoint a mutual friend who was dying of cancer. As we sat with this incredibly faithful servant of life and love, I was experiencing a push and pull. There was sadness and joy, anger and gratitude, emptiness and fulfillment. Emotions were running rampant, and I felt as though that time together was a roller coaster ride through a very dark tunnel.

Upon returning home, I sobbed as I played the piano for a good while. And then, without even looking at a clock, I said to myself that it was time to shower and put the day and my friend to rest in my mind. And I did just that.

No one can understand death. No one can explain death. Regardless of what well-intentioned ministers will offer up as attempts at comfort, death is anything but comfortable. And a roller coaster ride through the shadows of darkness is anything but exciting.

For death is the end. Whether we image the after-death as a reincarnation or heaven, dining with a rich Lazarus or the 8th day, it's still the imagination. We use images because we need something to help us through the dark, knowing that there is no certainty of what is to come after death.

This is why religious language has us live by faith and not by sight, with an abiding trust and not with sensory knowledge.

Such abiding trust has an opposing voice. The spiritual hunger for wholeness cannot be satisfied in this world, and we are forever yearning for something more. Thus, we long for the fullness of life even as we hold on to the limitations of human existence.

These bells of human longing ring most shallow for those who are at death's door, who while yearning for something more are never really ready to leave what they have.

Few of us welcome the Angel of Death. We'd much rather tell him to return at a later date, when we are more available.

Still alive and in fairly good health, I can't imagine what it must be like to be anointed and have family members gathered at my side, waiting for the end of my life on this earth.

But I can say that I've experienced death. Even though not physically, I have died many times in life. I have gone through many chapters, many relationships, many deaths, many losses. And so have you, if you have been fully alive.

Divorce is a visit by the Angel of Death. As is being fired at Christmas or losing a loved one in January. These experiences are filled with a suffering that cannot and should not be fixed with medication. They must be lived through, not flown over.

There are other doors upon which the Angel of Death

knocks, doors that once opened can lead to a much more contented and fulfilled way of living; doors that give us hope that once opened, we will find on the other side a glimpse not of the Angel of Death, but of Heaven itself.

These are angels who knock on the doors of a meaningless existence, angels that help us see the ruts we have fallen into. They awaken us to the realization that our drive to success has left us with money but no one with whom to share, points of no return when total apathy and surrender overwhelm us, experiences whereby we simply do not care for anyone or anything.

The Angel of Death is near when we realize we have valued everyone else above our own lives and that life as we have known it is filled with false guilt and needless shame.

The Angel of Death comes in the fear that we have been abandoned by the Living God, rejected by life itself. He comes in the wake-up call we get that alerts us to all of the spending we've done for approval from people we don't even care about. He comes through the opportunity to catch ourselves once again leaving our bodies and longing to be somewhere else, anywhere but here.

These, too, are visits of the Angel of Death. They come for a good reason. They come because without such sobering visits, without such breakdowns, without surrender of one's way of living, we cannot move into the mystery of the beyond. The trees are barren as a sign that we, too, must let leaves fall from our yesterdays. For we can only experience new life when we have left the old behind.

Addicts know this all too well. We must give up our best friend in order to find a new one. That is much easier said than done when the friend has been faithful for so many years.

Paul Tillich (1886-1965), a German-American Christian existentialist philosopher and theologian who is widely regarded as one of the most influential theologians of the 20th century, says it best. Therefore, I leave you with his words in the hope that we all see more clearly that the Angel of Death may, in fact, be Grace.

From his *The Shaking of the Foundations*:

"Grace strikes us when we are in great pain and restlessness. It strikes us when we walk through the dark valley of a meaningless and empty life. It strikes us when we feel that our separation is deeper than usual because we have violated another life, a life which we loved or from which we were estranged. It strikes us when our disgust for our own being, our indifference, our weakness, our hostility and our lack of direction has become intolerable to us.

"It strikes us when, year after year, the longed-for perfection of life does not appear, when the old compulsions reign within us as they have for decades, when despair destroys all joy and courage. Sometimes, at that moment, a wave of light breaks into our darkness, and it is as though a voice was saying: 'You are accepted, accepted by that which is greater than you, and the name of which you do not know. Do not try to do anything now; perhaps later you will do much. Do not seek for anything, do not perform anything, do not intend anything. Simply accept the fact that you are accepted!'

"If that happens to us, we experience grace. After such an

experience, we may not be better than before, and we may not believe more than before, but everything is transformed … and nothing is demanded of this experience, no religious or moral or intellectual presupposition, nothing but acceptance."

The Waiting Game

"Whatever we may think about the human propensity to control one's destiny, the reality is that we are not in control of anything other than our responses to this game we call waiting."

Over the past several weeks, much of my spare time has been spent in hospitals. My 87-year-old father is suffering from many complications, not the least of which is the fact that his body is just giving out.

But who knows what the future holds. He may bounce back on his ninth life; he may be picked up by the chariots and carried across the River Jordan; he may be alive and waiting for the chariots to be brought down.

Whatever the case, one thing appears certain: Life is a waiting game. And the clock of life has very little, if any, predictability.

There are many time zones on this earth, and I'm not just talking about Central and Pacific. There is chronological time, hospital time, Mother Nature time, doctor office time and ER time.

There is dating time, romance time, times of surrender, times when adrenalin floods the circuits and times when we simply don't care anymore.

So many time zones in life.

And with all of these time zones comes the reality that we are more often than not waiting for something: waiting on the bus, waiting on the salad, waiting for a table, waiting for the report, waiting for the oil change to be completed, waiting for the interview, waiting for the divorce to be final, waiting on a text, waiting on a call from a friend.

Whatever we may think about the human propensity to control one's destiny, the reality is that we are not in control of anything other than our responses to this game we call waiting.

Yes, we are active in our life's goals, and many of us are pro-active in facing the challenges before they become insurmountable. But regardless of how much we strive to maintain control over our circumstances, the paradox is that we are more often out in front of them. We spend more time waiting for our lives to catch up than we do chasing it down. Such is the human condition.

The great line from one of my favorite movies, *Silver Lining Playbook,* says it best. "I've loved you since the day I met you. It just took me a while to catch up. I got stuck."

It seems to me that so much of life is either getting stuck, trying to get unstuck or waiting on a higher power to unstuck us!

We get stuck in our stubborn attitudes, presuppositions, life strategies, ego-centered directives and outdated patterns. It's as if we're always having to wait, not so patiently, I might add, for life to give us what it wants.

And we wait with boxing gloves on because in the depths of our consciousness, something much larger than our freedom seems to be calling the plays. And we don't like it. We'd rather be our captain, our director, our pilot, our designer. Surrender is not much fun. Neither is waiting.

As a nation, we are adept at demeaning procrastination as

anathema to our victory-driven society when what we truly need is to give it new meaning. Waiting is not a definitive curse placed upon us. It is often the very essence of mental and spiritual health.

To wait is to place our trust in what we cannot see. To wait is to sit on the bench and enjoy the passers-by and realize that life is a gift to receive and not a trophy to be chased. Therefore, procrastination may be waiting patiently, not putting off action. Maybe, just maybe, waiting is the best form of action at any given time.

We did a lot of waiting in the hospital, and it gave me much time to reflect on what it meant to be powerless over time, particularly my time zone that had me stuck in my own selfish desires for my father.

As I sat with a man crippled by his infections and returning masses of potential cancer, he seemed to be waiting. I just watched him. Sometimes his appearance was not so patient; at other times, it was purely serene.

As I waited, I would nap at times, read some magazines, ponder over the psalms or stare into space along with my father, waiting for the next gift God would be bringing.

Waiting doesn't mean passively resigning oneself to fate or concluding that life is meaningless. Nor does it mean giving up. Put simply, waiting is accepting ourselves as humble servants of a greater power, riding on a train that offers no reservations or timed stops. It means we are given over to a clock that, at times, seems to be stretching our imagination as did the old television show Twilight Zone and at other times, pulling heart strings through the romantic song *Twilight Time*.

Waiting is one of the greatest gifts life has given us, and it may be the very power that can un-stuck us. What an irony, huh? Waiting is what gives us the power to do.

Waiting affects our speech and avoids the utterance of destructive words toward another when we are in a defensive mode.

Waiting offers a quiet time to reflect upon the significance of life events, giving us perspective as to what is important and what is trivial.

Waiting supplies a portrait of life that allows for coloring outside the box of our deceptive emotions.

Waiting supplies us with the reality check that time zones are real, God's time is not our time and that living in the now doesn't mean I will get what I want.

Waiting is the most powerful anti-urgency pill on the market.

To say "we're waiting" is sometimes all we have at our disposal.

And yet, it's so very difficult to wait. We change lanes on the interstate, we change lines in grocery stores, we jump to conclusions before the person has finished speaking, we anticipate a preemptive strike by someone we distrust and build a wall to protect ourselves. We jump the nurses when they are not right there when we call. We grab the most current financially lucrative offer without waiting for other factors to be brought into view. We go for the instant pleasure even as we know that to delay gratification, to wait, is to turn the key toward peace.

All because we are stuck in our fear, quick-sanded in our securities, frozen in our past movies that continue to threaten us. Rational or not, threats to safety are real. And waiting is one giant threat to safety.

Could there be a time zone in which we courageously sat in silence and overpowered the perceived threats with acceptance that life is our best friend?

Could there be a time zone in which we transcend the mere tolerating of long lines, begrudgingly putting up with life's intrusions, bitterly swallowing unanswered prayers and begin to live the waiting game with joy, gratitude and anticipation?

Could there be a time zone in our human journey where powerlessness is promoted to wisdom and brute force is deleted as a word from our personal mind computers?

Could there be a time zone in which we truly live in such a way that we ask for love's will to be done, not ours?

As I looked at my father over these past few weeks of suffering, I became more humbled with every hour that passed. He lay there, dependent upon others to feed him, bathe him, clothe him, clean him and, at times, push him to help himself in whatever manner he could.

He waited. I waited. Life itself even seemed to be waiting. At times, it was painful; at other times, peaceful. I was unable to choose the one that would bring me the most fulfillment. It was all so unclear. Why? Because life is a mixture of both.

Time stood still, and the rain was all we could hear through the window of the little room. I imagined the chariots waiting to be sent, the angels waiting to escort, the bands waiting to play and the crowds of history waiting to cheer.

Waiting. Sometimes, it's all we can do. Sometimes, it's the best that life has to offer.

Joseph Campbell is quoted as saying, "We have to let go of the life we have planned so as to accept the one that is waiting for us."

I say that sometimes, we have to wait with palms open in order to receive what is coming to us.

The Gift of Grief

"Grief... is a time for cleaning out the clutter and washing the windows of life so that we can see more clearly and breathe more easily."

Mary Oliver tells us, "To live in this world, you must be able to do three things: to love what is mortal, to hold it against your bones knowing your own life depends on it and, when the time comes, to let it go."

My daddy gifted me with his death on February 18, 2014.

A gift that allows both the absence and presence of mind to comingle.

Death is not just the loss of another. It is the loss of mind, of soul, of spirit, of meaning. But it is also the gaining of new opportunities and perspectives, strength of character and self-respect. Death allows us to defy all logic and be present to the dust to which we shall all return.

When the gift of death strikes the core of our being and we are wrenching from the loss of part of our soul, if we are real, we open ourselves to mystery and move from our human time zone into a space where gravity takes over.

Grief is a gift that awakens in us a need for quiet time, reflection and solitude to sift through memories and come to grips with what has happened to us.

Grief awakens in us a need to reject outright those who out of their own insecurity attempt to sidestep the pain through phrases like, "He's in a better place." On the other hand, we are just as profoundly possessed by a powerful force that helps us resist lashing out at those who mean well but who are unable to understand the emptiness. Or who have not the strength to face their own soon-to-be.

Grief awakens anger and a hurt that cannot be hospitalized, biopsied, cured with antibiotics or surgically removed. We enter a crazy time of raw rage, when we are at the same time angry with the one who left us and even more so at life itself for giving us the gift of love and then asking us to let it go. We enter a period of deep distrust and cynicism.

Grief awakens a recovery: a time when we reevaluate the "what" and the "who" that can be relied upon. Who is significant to our redemption; those who nourish us, who intoxicate us, who use us, who give to us the essentials of true love, who allow us to expose the ugliness of death without shaming us, who respect our disbelief and apathy. It is a time when, in the midst of loss, we can honestly appraise our lives and future investments of our limited time on this earth.

Grief awakens an acceptance of the limitations of humanity. Through our loss, we come to more fully appreciate how messy life is, how broken and hypocritical we all are, how limited and impure human love is, and how people are at times unavailable when we need them most.

Grief awakens the age-old question, "What's it all about?" and beckons us to live peacefully within the doubt and meaningless existence in order that something larger than our visions, plans and dreams may provide a new meaning to life.

Grief awakens a season to reset the boundaries of what's acceptable and what's not, whom we'll carry and whom we will not, whom we can share our values with and whom we cannot. It is a time for cleaning out the clutter and washing the windows of life so that we can see more clearly and breathe more easily.

All these awakenings, all these seasons, all these time zones of grief entangled like Christmas lights that can only be untangled with patience and gentle pacing. And even when we begin to untangle the wires of grief, we find our wires moving in so many more directions with no certainty of where we will be transported.

Hope is perhaps trusting that while we are untangling it all, we are being transported back into the arms of love; ironically, the very arms that we felt dropped us when we lost our beloved.

But then what else is there? What other arms are there but the arms that unfold before us each day when we awaken and ask us to be carried by a power greater than our own needs and wants?

What else is there than to return to the arms that both hold and let go? That both protect and wound? That both seduce and betray?

It may sound cynical to trust in love again after watching a loved one slowly fade into the night and do so with the sobering realization that "I am the only one I will never love or leave." But it is authentic, if nothing else. And it is worth it.

Years ago, when I was in treatment for severe depression and wanted to die, one of the rituals in the group was for the other six men to seek my trust. I was to fall backwards, hoping they would hold and rest me in their locked arms.

Once in their arms, they gently rocked me back and forth as if I were an infant.

It was one of the most powerful experiences of my life. When I was put down, the therapist asked me what I experienced. The memory is vivid. I tearfully said that it wasn't only the assurance of things unseen. It was also the reality that I couldn't be held forever and that I wanted to rest as long as I could with gratitude.

These men loved this broken man back to life through a gesture of simple holding and gentle rocking and then put me down and asked me to learn to rock myself.

My daddy rocked me to sleep each night when I was a child, and as these men were rocking me in 1993, I recalled how much we all long to be held. To this very day, I love rocking myself into a quiet zone.

One recent night, when I returned home from a long day of counseling, I rocked and rocked, slowing my flood of emotions, and asked God to quiet my mind that I might also have a time for rest and restoration.

I slowly faded out, much the same way my father fell into eternal rest. The only difference was that we awakened to a different time zone.

His zone is now eternal rest, eternal peace, eternal love and eternal light. Mine is limited.

Therefore, there are but three things I ask of the Lord of Life through this gift of grief: that I continue to love what is mortal, hold that love against my bones believing my life depends on it and, when the time comes, let it go.

The Murder of Matthew Shepard

"Family values have nothing to do with whether one is gay or straight. They have everything to do with sharing one's resources, bearing one another's burdens, supporting each other during times of need."

On October 7, 1998, two men led Matthew Shepard to a remote area where they commited unimaginable acts of hate. Tied to a split-rail fence where he was beaten, robbed and left to die in the cold of the night, Matthew suffered for nearly 18 hours before being discovered. On October 12, 1998, the young gay man died.

All these many years later, we still struggle with sexual orientation. Despite the rapidly changing poll numbers favoring equal rights, the acceptance of gay rights by a prominent U.S. Senator whose son came out and the cease-fire called for by the Pope, gays and lesbians still fight for their dignity in a nation that calls itself the land of opportunity.

In a land whose constitution begs for life, liberty and equal pursuit of happiness, our schools continue to be plagued by bullying, our adolescents continue to see suicide as a viable option to ease the pain of daily exclusion and our parents continue to either deny its presence in their households or become so embroiled in what the neighbors will think that they can't see the agony in their own children.

As a mental health professional, I see it all, from the rage of a 40-year-old man just coming to terms with his orientation to the depression of a young adult who spent her high school years hiding behind books and computers, terrified that someone might find out she liked other girls. I have the challenge of assisting them rediscover their dignity, find forgiveness in their hearts and create purpose beyond their own internalized homophobia. In other words, most of these wounded children of God have learned to hate themselves.

All the while that I am working to help these hurting members of our society form self-respect, surrounding me are Christians who either cast same-sex-oriented people into the fires of hell or, even worse, accept the sinner but not the sin, which is another way of saying you can think gay, feel gay and even desire love with another man, just don't allow it to enter into your daily living. Believing that one can fake it 'til they make it, these fear-mongering attitudes fuel the status quo, lest our society's fabric be torn to shreds.

All who indulge themselves in the thinking that one man, one woman is the only path to truth have themselves been so brainwashed that they can't see that one of their very own may be suffering: perhaps a brother, a sister, a son or daughter, a niece or nephew. Nor do they see that poverty is increasing, the rich are getting richer at the expense of the poor, we are being taxed to death, addiction suffocates the ability to express genuine love, our government has become an army and an insurance company and that our children are going to bed hungry. Purity laws are often simpler to understand than the challenges of real social justice, even when behind closed doors, we are anything but pure.

We have become so terrified of gays being recognized as legitimate children of God and not intrinsically evil that we can't see the forest for the trees. So, we see a tree that is different from the rest and name it the enemy of a healthy society, avoiding the real issues that plague us. As a people, we continue to make accusations that being gay destroys family values and leads to a society devoid of morals: all of this coming from a population that has as its track record a divorce rate that tops 50 percent. So much for one man, one woman.

Organizations that control the microphone cry out that acceptance of homosexuality could lead to further atrocities against traditional marriage, frightening the ignorant masses towards pointing fingers at those who have done nothing more than be themselves. As a Christian and an entrenched Catholic, my pain is split: I hurt for the sons and daughters and their parents who come to my office begging for help. But I equally grieve for those who are so frightened of any other form of love that they unwittingly fuel the flames of violence and discrimination.

I am hurt that so many religious leaders in our community are silent when it comes to the greatest commandment: to love thy neighbor as thyself. I am pained that we skirt the elephants in so many rooms of our homes, pretending that it would never happen "in my family." I am appalled that the followers of family values, with their insistence on traditional marriage, overlook justice, charity, unconditional love and humility and that ministers of good will continue to avoid calling out the sin of judging others, particularly those others who are gay, lesbian, bisexual or transgendered.

Family values have nothing to do with whether one is gay or straight. They have everything to do with sharing one's resources, bearing one another's burdens, supporting each other during times of need. They have to do with visiting prisoners, putting up with acne and awkward social skills, showing compassion for those who are sick and honoring the dead. Family values have to do with standing tall against those who would scapegoat others rather than look into their own sinful lives; with loving the poor, marginalized and dispossessed; with having the courage to challenge any degradation of another human person; with showing gratitude for one's life without frills or objects of pleasure; with respecting earth and all of its inhabitants, from the fish in the sea to the birds in the air. Family values have to do with a father saying to his gay son, "You are my son, and nothing will ever separate us."

In an age of such knowledge and awareness, who could be more dispossessed than those who still hide their true selves in closets of fear and who walk into dark bars in order to find some sense of community; those who marry in order to fit in, who live lives of secrecy and duplicity; those who are so fearful of rejection that they can't tell their parents or best friends who they really are. Equal in dignity to all those in traditional marriages but who have to hide are those same-sex couples who ask for nothing more than the right to live free from a foundation of eggshells and to be welcomed at the national family table.

If Jesse Jackson can say that African-Americans catch the early bus to work, I can say that some of the very tax dollars contributed to that bus come from hard-working gays and lesbians, citizens who pay the same taxes as anyone else.

Jesus was concerned that we share our coats with those who have not even one. He was concerned that we not become plastered to the walls of purity but that we live lives filled with love for the least among us.

One can quote all the scripture passages one wants to against homosexuality. They will never change my conscience, which tells me without a doubt that the true harbors of hate, the real destroyers of morality, are those attitudes which would deny people the chance to live productive and fulfilling love, whether between men or between women, by judging them unnatural.

Perhaps what saddens me most as I reflect on when Matthew Shepard was found is the statement of the cyclist who found him. He thought he was looking at a scarecrow. It's too fitting an image to go unnoticed. There are far too many beautiful people waiting to have their voices fully heard, their gifts fully received, their hearts ready to lend a hand towards a more perfect union but who are still seen as scarecrows.

The time has come for those who also profess Christianity to stand and speak. No more discrimination, no more war on homosexuality, no more hatred and scapegoating by the vocal few whose existence seems to depend more on keeping the wars alive than on achieving true peace and harmony. May we never forget the message of He who offered His life: "Love one another as I have loved you."

Technology Has Gone Public: Now What?

"There is a huge difference between secrecy and privacy, and we need to be discerning those differences both within and in the public forum."

In case you haven't heard, technology has gone public.

Yes, we can Skype with friends in Japan, send out group texts and emails and keep people aware of our current location. We can post pictures instantly, video fathers singing to their children and tweet our musings for the world, limited only by the number of letters, not people.

The problem with going public is that there is no discrimination. And so the search for intimacy, for closeness, has taken a shotgun approach: the reach of which extends beyond even our wildest imaginings.

And so, with the speed of light, the social networks wield a power to destroy as well as create, to invade as well as inform, to cripple human dignity as well as advance human progress.

The screens are down, and we have become infatuated with this apparent freedom to allow the world to know our every personal act or thought.

Someone recently expressed to me, "Through texting, I find myself expressing what I would never consider in person-to-person conversation."

All too often, I hear what appears to be a blatant dismissal of human capability to discern technological usage when it's said that in today's age, there is no such thing as privacy. As if we have given in to our creations without And yet, this speaks to a truth I care not to accept. With every technological advance, we have become closer to each other. Fire brought us closer. Wheels brought us closer. Then there was the telegraph and the telephone. The list goes on. So the question is asked, how close is too close? And what happens to the human person when the closet is opened for the world to see?

It is ironic that through instant messages and texting with people we don't know, we act as if the anonymous and impersonal provides privacy. But in reality, it gives birth to a secret self; and a secret self has a hard time remaining in the closet, especially when everyone has access to the home. And that's what the present age offers. Anyone at any time can get into our private lives, our personal homes. What was intended as my little secret has now become available for the world to view.

However, there is another side to human dignity that is not secretive. In looking for a moment of pleasure and escape from the ordinary through secrecy, we overlook what we truly need: privacy.

We long for privacy as much as we long for intimacy, for the right to be out of our ordinary structure, away from the 24/7 mentality, out of the persona, dressed down, unscreened in word and deed, able to be without make up or hair pieces or shaved legs. We need the ability to stuff the closets when friends come for dinner, knowing that they will not be opened. And if they were opened by the guest, rude and impolite they would be considered, scratched from the list of those welcomed to the next dinner party.

The same can be said for private space to recreate.

Psychologists call "liminal space" a place where boundaries dissolve a little and we stand there, on the threshold, getting ourselves ready to move across the limits of what we were into what we are to be.

It represents a period of ambiguity, of marginality and transition.

Humans need moments of liminality, times we call a recess, a break, a relaxation moment or engagement in matters that promote neither fame nor infamy. It's getting away from as much as it is going toward.

How many of us go to Las Vegas? New York? The beach? All places that are out of our ordinary structure. We go for the expressed reason of rejuvenating ourselves, and we believe we are within the confines of our personal privacy.

If we're honest with ourselves, we would readily admit that we don't want to see anyone we know. Not because we are ashamed. We simply want privacy.

We say with no regret that adolescents need their doors closed at times, that healthy relationships promote rights based in trust and respect for the other's privacy. We tell children that there are private parts of their bodies that are not to be touched. And we offer the 5th amendment, through which one's privacy, at least until counsel is retained, can be shielded from self-recrimination.

There is a huge difference between secrecy and privacy, and we need to be discerning those differences both within and in the public forum.

For secrecy starves the soul while privacy feeds it.

The advances of communication have brought us yet to another crossroads for humanity. We can take this crisis as an opportunity to feed or to starve.

As always, the choice lies in human hands.

Film Not Made for the Theater

*"I cannot change what happened on that fateful night;
nor can I change the sensationalizing of a tragedy.
But I can change the channel."*

Leaving my office on July 20, 2012, I heard about the theater shootings in Aurora, Colorado, and offered a silent prayer for the dead, the survivors, all those who were in the theater and, of course, the gunman and his family. Ever since hearing once that Judas had a mother, I have been aware that violent actions come from people who themselves were once children.

I went about my regular schedule and avoided the news, which I knew would be a 24-hour invasion by the media into the lives of persons of interest. I spent a few minutes of that afternoon making a banana pudding for my neighbors. In my sadness, I needed to take some kind of action, and remembering how my mother would make the family this wonderful dessert each Sunday, it seemed most appropriate to call upon her spirit and do something with my anger and feelings of powerlessness.

It wasn't until the following Sunday morning when I broke down a bit in what I hope was a genuine human response to reading the names of those whose lives were ended without warning or warrant. Tears surfaced as I was confronted with the reality of a 6 year old's death and her injured mother's constant request of caregivers for a report on her daughter's condition.

Sunday evening, as I turned on the television to catch a glimpse of the day's news, admittedly having forgotten about the tragedy, I was bombarded by the drama of interviews with family members, investigations into the shooter's past and questions to patients who were no doubt traumatized by the event as to whether they would forgive the person responsible. There is simply no other way to put it than to say that once again, I felt deterred and distracted, not by the hopes and dreams of democracy, but by the hype and hypertension of obsession.

Now I know better what it means to say curiosity killed the cat.

The television was turned off, and I went to pull weeds in the garden to calm and distract myself. As I worked, the serenity prayer became my alternative to the drug of curiosity that was knocking on every door and window of my internal home. "Give me the serenity to accept what I cannot change, the courage to change what I can and the wisdom to know the difference."

I cannot change what happened on that fateful night; nor can I change the sensationalizing of a tragedy. But I can change the channel. I can change my mood of disgust with what has often taken a paparazzi approach to news. So I spent the remainder of the evening with everything turned off, even the lights, and I asked God for serenity, courage and wisdom.

And here's what I received:

While I have no power over another person's actions,
- I can and will continue to speak out against assault weapons in the hands of the public. No one will convince me that we have a right to such guns.
- I can and will continue to trust that the vast majority of citizens are both law abiding and decent in their treatment of one another.

- I can and will continue to challenge our public appetite for sensationalism as an escape from our personal responsibility to promote safety in our local communities.
- I can and will continue to advocate for violence prevention at all levels, including domestic abuse, bullying and discrimination.
- I can and will continue to strive for empathy, compassion and validation towards each person I come in contact with on a daily basis, providing attention that rewards the higher self in each of us.
- I can and will continue to do what I can to eradicate poverty, ignorance, self-loathing, unemployment and internalized shame.
- I can and will continue to speak out against any cable news marketing and advertising strategies that promote drama addiction, invasion of privacy and slanted commentary while demoting good news.
- I can and will continue to think globally and act locally, focusing my attention not on "out or over there" but on "right here, right now."
- I can and will continue to believe that mental disease and spiritual darkness are two sides of the same coin and that I live to promote both healthy minds and healthy souls.
- I can and will continue to believe that violent actions are reflections of a violent internal home and that peace will only come when we put down the weapons of self-hatred and fear of self.
- I can and will continue to promote human dignity as the standard to which all religious dialogue must be held, intervening whenever self-righteousness is postured.

There is no doubt that the shooting has impacted me,

saddened me and, at the same time, bolstered me. It's time that we turned off the television, YouTube and the internet more often and, as my mother would say, "put our hands in the dirt or the cake bowl. Either one will help us reach out beyond despair and help us maintain our power for good."

On that very evening, after turning off the television and working in the yard, I received a picture of my neighbor's daughter eating the banana pudding, and I smiled.

And at that moment, my balloon of life was filled again.

Rights and Responsibilities

"...in the end, we truly are separate while equal, individual yet interconnected."

Newton Minow once said, "We've gotten to the point where everybody's got a right and nobody's got a responsibility."

While we can certainly debate what constitutes legitimate entitlement and what pathways lead to genuine self-esteem, the fact that we have rights as well as responsibilities is universally accepted. Under scrutiny, the two worlds are inextricably bound together, and the notion of "I" versus "us" is a false dichotomy. There can be no self-esteem or entitlement without responsibility for a greater good.

All too often in the world of behavioral health, while applauding the construction of personal rights and emotional boundaries, we are tempted to overlook the reality that we are responsible for our actions even when our rights are violated and our boundaries are crossed. In **Rethinking Rights and Responsibilities: The Moral Bonds of Community**, author Arthur J. Dyck stated, "Strengthening rights is dependent on strengthening the connections, conceptually and behaviorally, between rights and responsibilities."

His insight leads me to wonder about the language of personal rights. The notion of "I" language, while often appropriate, needs to be distinguished between "we each," especially when a greater connection is sought. Therefore, I offer the following list of personal responsibilities as well as personal rights, not as "I" but as "we each," implying that in the end, we truly are separate while equal, individual yet interconnected.

We each:
- have the right to make a request for something and the responsibility to live at peace without its acquisition.
- have the right to prefer one over another and the responsibility to live happily without our preferences.
- have the right to choose our behaviors and the responsibility to think through the effects of our actions on others.
- have the right so say no and the responsibility to be reasonable when doing so.
- have the right to refuse a request without guilt and the responsibility to allow others do the same.
- have the right to be assertive, even when another's feelings are hurt, as long as we did not violate the other's human rights and the responsibility to allow others the same rights.
- have the right to commit by saying yes and the responsibility to follow through on that commitment.
- have the right to say I'm not sure and the responsibility to follow up with an answer within a reasonable time frame.
- have the right to change our decisions, direction and thoughts and the responsibility to make those changes, not from avoidance of, but rather toward the betterment of self and the world.
- have the right to make mistakes and the responsibility to not only learn from but also to avoid making them again.
- have the right to prioritize our values and the responsibility to accept that at times, values will clash and judgment calls will have to be made.
- have the right to verbally express our values and the responsibility to live them out in our daily actions.
- have the right to ambivalent feelings and the

responsibility to seek resolve.
- have the right to become our highest selves and the responsibility to draw forth the same from others.
- have the right to assert discomfort when behaviors conflict with our values and the responsibility to express that discomfort with respect.
- have the right to express our religious beliefs and the responsibility to respect those of others.
- have the right to disallow certain actions/behaviors/attitudes in our home and the responsibility to display proper etiquette within the homes of others.
- have to the right to limit our availability to the needs of others and the responsibility to trust that their needs can get met through a power greater than self.
- have the right to expect honesty and the responsibility to be honest in all of our dealings.
- have the right to be angry at someone and the responsibility to avoid violating that person's dignity.
- have the right to privacy and the responsibility to avoid secrecy.
- have the right to be unique and the responsibility to accept our commonality.
- have the right to be listened to and taken seriously and the responsibility to listen to others.
- have the right to uncertainty and the responsibility to express it without shame.
- have the right to choose those in whom we wish to confide and the responsibility to treat all others with dignity and civility.
- have the right to be trusted and the responsibility to be trustworthy.
- have the right to be playful and the responsibility to fair play.
- have the right to personal space and time and the responsibility to care for it wisely.

- have the right to be healthy and the responsibility to avoid self-righteousness.
- have the right to feel safe in an environment and the responsibility to provide others safety when in our presence.
- have the right to stretch our minds and bodies and the responsibility to accept the limits of aging.
- have the right to be treated with respect and the responsibility to return the favor.
- have the right to feel sad, mad and glad and the responsibility to live with the belief that this, too, shall pass.
- have the right to stewardship of each day and the responsibility to spend it wisely.
- have the right to compassion and empathy from others and the responsibility to express it toward others.
- have the right to intimacy and the responsibility to treat our life companion with respect.
- have the right to be fearful and the responsibility to face fears with courage.
- have the right to ask for help and the responsibility to help others.
- have the right to work and the responsibility to be competent, effective and efficient.
- have the right to fair treatment and the responsibility to assert injustice without degradation.
- have the right to speak and the responsibility to listen.
- have the right to disagree with an opinion and the responsibility to defend another's right to express it.
- have the right to forgive ourselves, knowing that we are evolving, and the responsibility to forgive those who have offended us with the same underlying assumption.

A Bucket List That Will Change Your Life

"A college psychology professor once told me that we don't see the world objectively. We read the world subjectively."

Ever since Morgan Freeman and Jack Nicholson lit up the screen with the film, people are often asked the question, What's on your bucket list? What do you want to do before you die?

How about we ask something similar as we reach the end of our reflections? What's in the bucket list of service that could help us read the world differently?

For those who are attempting to do without alcohol, he or she is told, "Do 90 meetings in 90 days."

For those wanting to start exercising, we say, Whatever it is one chooses to do, do it for three weeks. And it becomes a habit.

For those who want to remove negative self-talk, we advise recitation of positive messages throughout the day that change the existing tapes that are on autopilot.

A college psychology professor once told me that we don't see the world objectively. We read the world subjectively. It has stuck with me since the tender age of 19.

And so I ask of us, as we come to the end of our reflections, to think about how we read the world and how might we wish to read it differently.

Or put another way, where do we walk during the day? How do we behave in ways we wish to change? What attitudes seem to weigh us down? What relationship patterns do we know need to be redesigned?

During a recent conversation, a friend suggested that true conversion is not about moving from the head to the heart; rather, it is about moving from the mouth to the foot. What we say needs to be consistent with how we behave.

Pretty simple, huh?

Here's a beginning list of actions we might could take that could, when done habitually, sincerely, open-mindedly and respectfully, change the way we read the world and, therefore, make the soil of the earthly soul a bit more fertile.

1. Enter into another person's culture and show gratitude for what they offer the world.

2. Enter into another religious expression and show gratitude for how they worship.

3. Mentor one person who is in need of assistance.

4. Call a different person from your past each day for 90 days.

5. Read a book that challenges your worldview.

6. Take the bus or some form of public transit that is traditionally populated by the poor and listen to the story of someone you sit next to.

7. Give up a pleasure for 40 days and put the money toward a favorite cause.

8. Write down five experiences a night for which you are grateful from the preceding 24 hours.

9. Send a handwritten note daily to someone whom you respect, and point out what their life has meant to you.

10. Join a group that interests you and stretches your imagination.

11. Learn some form of art from a professional in that field, be it learning to play a musical instrument, painting, sculpture, ballet or swing.

12. Put your hands into the dirt on a regular basis, and watch either the plants or the flowers grow.

13. When possible, take the day off when it's raining, and sit quietly listening to the sounds and watching the earth drink the water of life.

14. Start a monthly book study group, and allow each member to pick a book for all to read and discuss.

15. Keep a journal and record creative thoughts, insights, ah-ha moments and forgotten memories.

16. Smile at every person you meet on the street; wave at every person you see from your car; look in the eye of every customer service agent you engage with and ask, "How are you doing today? Thank you for what you do for us each day."

17. Make amends with a childhood neighbor, elementary school teacher whom you felt were unfair, bullies who mistreated you, family members who shamed you.

18. Write a letter to the universe, and ask to be released from the burdensome memories of past offenses, strained relationships, bitter rivalries, jealous comparisons, self-aggrandizement, betrayals of trust and the lack of genuine self-respect – from which all offenses have risen.

19. Show kindness to every living creature, from humans who wish to do you harm to dogs who only wish to follow you around. See the Divine in all creation and afford it the same dignity that you give yourself.

20. Set aside a time each morning to be grateful for what will come your way and a time each evening to reflect on the goodness of life.